Practice Leadership in the
Early Years

T0368848

Practice Leadership in the Early Years
Becoming, Being and Developing as a Leader

*Mark Hadfield, Michael Jopling and
Martin Needham*

 Open University Press

Open University Press
McGraw-Hill Education
McGraw-Hill House
Shoppenhangers Road
Maidenhead
Berkshire
England
SL6 2QL

email: enquiries@openup.co.uk
world wide web: www.openup.co.uk

and Two Penn Plaza, New York, NY 10121–2289, USA

First published 2015

A catalogue record of this book is available from the British Library

ISBN–13: 978–0–33–526296–0 (pb)
ISBN–10: 0–33–526296–1 (pb)
eISBN: 978–0–33–526297–7

Library of Congress Cataloging-in-Publication Data
CIP data applied for

Typesetting and e-book compilations by
RefineCatch Limited, Bungay, Suffolk

Fictitious names of companies, products, people, characters and/or data that may be used herein (in case studies or in examples) are not intended to represent any real individual, company, product or event.

Printed and bound by CPI Group (UK) Ltd, Croydon, CR0 4YY

Praise for this book

"This book provides unique insights into Early Years 'practice leadership' and uses research to inform quality improvement. The authors set the scene with a review of policy and its effects on practice leadership, before combining key aspects emerging from their own research and wider theory with practical guidance on how to assess and improve practice leadership and quality Early Years provision. There is a strong focus on the relationships which support and develop inclusion and shared responsibility for creating a culture of change and improvement that include the perspectives of children and parents as equal partners. This book will be of value to all involved in Early Years practice and leadership as well as students at all levels and researchers."

Michael Gasper, Early Years Consultant

"The introduction of a graduate leader has been one of the most significant developments in early years in recent times. This book therefore provides essential reading for all 'leaders' in the early years especially those with Early Years Professional Status or currently undertaking Early Years Teacher Status (0–5). Drawing upon the longitudinal national evaluation of Early Years Professional Status, it provides clear evidence to support those in leadership roles to reflect upon and develop their practice. Most importantly it recognises that there is not one type of leader and that innovation occurs when the graduate leader is able to apply their professional training and experience to a specific setting."

Dr Eunice Lumsden, Head of Early Years,
The University of Northampton, UK

"This is a very timely, reflective, dynamic and informative book that is thought provoking and very much needed by practitioners, students, researchers, policy makers, service commissioners and those conducting regulatory work in the sector. At its heart and as a golden thread throughout is the authors' focus upon practice leadership as a means of getting it right for children and families and for practitioners and provisions in our sector too. The different views around what *constitutes quality provision are not shied away from and the exploration of consensus about what constitutes 'quality' provides much needed food for thought.*

The authors have produced a very valuable resource that will fundamentally assist with increasing understanding and with changing and enhancing leadership and collaborative service delivery practice in the sector."

Chrissy Meleady MBE, Early Years Equality and Equality and
Human Rights UK

Contents

Preface

Our aim in writing this book is not to produce another set of generalised characteristics of effective leaders in the early years, but rather to draw insights from our research into how to bring about change to support new and existing leaders as they try to make improvements to practice.

This book arises out of our research with 40 leaders in the early years sector in England who were part of a central government initiative, Early Years Professional Status (EYPS), designed to improve leadership in the sector. We followed these leaders for three years after they gained this status as they tried to enact in their own settings the initiative's aspirations for them to become 'change agents' and 'leaders of practice'. Through their successes and failures, we have been able to build up a picture of what it means to try to lead improvements in practice at a time of massive changes in the sector as it responded to growing external pressures and a range of new government initiatives.

In talking to these leaders and observing their work, we have developed our understanding of what it means to be a practice leader in the early years and what practice leadership entails. The combined impact of their training and external inspection and policy pressures means that our cohort of leaders focus much of their activities on developing practices in their setting that they believe will comply with the notions of quality to be found in inspection and curriculum guidelines and will hopefully have a positive impact on children. This book is therefore not about leadership in general or even leadership in the early years sector, rather it focuses on that strand of leaders' activities that is most concerned with improving practice and enhancing the quality of settings' provision. We called this strand 'practice leadership'.

This book is based around a set of four principles of practice that many of our leaders adopted as they set about their innovations. These principles provide basic guidance about what to do, but as the devil is often in the detail, it is these leaders' understanding of their settings that shaped their approach to leading specific innovations. We explore this idea of leaders' 'situational awareness' in our case studies and in the tools we provide in order to show that, although leaders should follow certain principles of practice, the most effective leaders adapt their approaches in response to the contexts in which they find themselves. Even more importantly, we argue that the most effective leaders adapt how they lead in response to changes in the capacity of their settings as new leaders emerge.

Acknowledgements

We would like to thank practice leaders and their colleagues in the 30 case study settings who were all so generous with their time during the research. We would also like to acknowledge the significant contribution made by Tim Waller, one of the directors of the original research team, and the other team members: Liz Coleyshaw, Mahmoud Emira, Karl Royle, Faye Stanley and Judy Whitmarsh.

Russell Goffe-Wood provided key design input and Julie Richmond-Lunn and Louise Clewer, along with other colleagues at the University of Wolverhampton, provided project management and administrative expertise. We would like to thank Ronnie Woods of the Enquire Learning Trust whose work on developing reflective learning processes we drew on in Chapter 7, Chris Pascal and Tony Bertram of CREC who advised on the research approach, and Tabetha Newman who advised on quantitative data analysis. Barbara Spender proofread the whole book and Sarah Barlow and Soundhouse Media created the films for the multimedia versions of the case studies in Chapter 5 that can be found at www.cedare-reports/eyps.

We acknowledge the support of the Children's Workforce Development Council, the Teaching Agency and the Department for Education, which commissioned and funded the research. We would particularly like to thank Thom Crabbe and the members of the funder's advisory group for their very useful advice and guidance throughout the research.

Please note that all names used in the book are pseudonyms.

Figures and tables

Figures

Tables

PART 1

1 The nature of leadership in the Early Years

In this chapter, we offer a critical introduction to those aspects of leadership research in the early years that shaped our approach to researching practice leadership. We argue that the notion of practice leadership arose out of a policy context concerned with improving the quality of overall provision and research on leadership effectiveness that attempted to link leaders' activities to improved outcomes for children. The impact of these two overlapping agendas has been to focus attention on those aspects of leadership most directly concerned with changing the practice of others in ways that were likely to improve the quality of provision and outcomes for children. It is these aspects we describe as practice leadership. However, it is important to emphasise that practice leadership is not just a confection of policy makers' concerns and effectiveness researchers' findings, it also arises from the professional concerns of practitioners in the early years sector who have taken on leadership roles. In a context characterised by a robust external inspection regime and debates over what constitutes high quality provision, these leaders have had to consider, more than ever in recent years, how to improve practice in their settings and what constitutes 'quality'. Practice leadership is, therefore, not a new form or style of leadership, but a constructed strand, or contested space, of leadership, bounded by the differing concerns and imperatives of policy makers, researchers and practitioners. Figure 1.1 attempts to represent diagrammatically how this strand is constructed.

The space created at the centre of this diagram effectively maps out the area of practice leadership, which has been the focus of so much policy and research interest. In this book, we draw on our own research into practice leadership from a somewhat different perspective to that of effectiveness researchers. This is because our research agenda was concerned less with identifying the generic practices that resulted in improved outcomes and more with how practitioners brought about improvements in their settings' quality of provision.

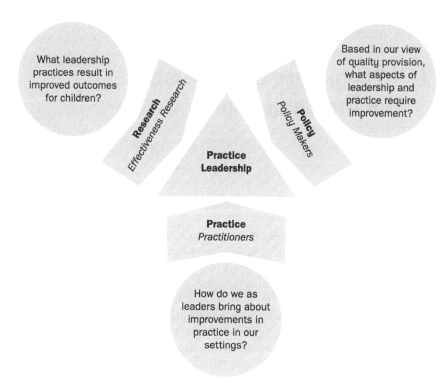

Figure 1.1 Constructing practice leadership.

Obviously, Figure 1.1 is a simplification of what is quite a contested space among policy makers, researchers and practitioners, in which arguments about what constitutes quality provision and how it can be brought about in the diverse settings and contexts that characterise the early years sector continue to rage.[1] In this chapter, we discuss the research and policies that framed our research interest as we started out on a three-year study of early years leaders. After outlining the policy context in which early years leadership has developed in England in recent years, we explore the emerging research consensus as to what constitutes effective leadership practices in early years settings.[2]

Our own research focused on a key policy initiative aimed at improving provision in the early years sector in England: the introduction of Early Years Professional Status (EYPS). The status was seen as a means of improving what later came to be termed 'practice leadership',[3] in effect leadership activity focused on improving the practice of others. Our research into early years leaders with EYPS is based on three-year longitudinal case studies of 30 settings and more than 40 leaders. These case studies combined objective measures of the quality of their provision with in-depth interviews and social network analysis to explore the relationship between the development of leadership capacity and improvements in provision. In policy terms at least, the launch of EYPS cemented the links between leadership, enhancing the quality of provision and improved outcomes for children and families. Later in this chapter we problematise these links as we discuss the complex nature of professional identity and collective agency. These ideas and the nature of the causal links between leaders' actions and improved outcomes for children are central to our discussion in the rest of this book.

Researching leadership in early education settings

The growing interest in leadership in early education in recent years has led to claims that there has been insufficient research in the area,[4] that the research has often not captured the depth and complexity of early years practice,[5] and that there has been relatively little training for and few expectations of leaders in early years.[6] However, there is broad agreement in the existing research literature about the wide range of roles and structures that exist in the sector[7] and, while profitable use has been made of elements of school leadership research, these structures and circumstances are sufficiently complex, and different from school contexts, to warrant a distinct research agenda.

Our overall approach to studying early years leadership is founded on our attempts to counter what have been regarded as some of the main limitations of this research: its failure to adequately capture how leadership in early years settings is enacted and develops over time,[8] and how it is responsive to the settings in which it is located. These limitations arise because much of the previous research has relied on surveys and interviews with leaders that explored their day-to-day roles, responsibilities and characteristics, rather than observing their leadership practices and relationships with others,[9] or it was based on the relatively limited perspective of a single leader or project.[10]

A great deal of the research that has explored the link between effective leadership and improvements in quality has built on the evidence provided by the influential Effective Provision of Pre-School Education (EPPE) project.[11] A key finding of EPPE was that the qualifications and experience of the person responsible for leading practice in the setting make a difference to the quality of children's experiences in their setting and their achievements up to the end of primary school (at least). In their follow-on project, the Effective Leadership in the Early Years Study (ELEYS), Siraj-Blatchford and Manni (2007) compared the characteristics of leaders in a group of 12 settings that had excellent outcomes to the characteristics of leaders in the other 129 EPPE study settings.[12] They highlighted the link between quality, in terms of outcomes for children and strong leadership, and a graduate teacher workforce that engages with curriculum issues. These findings were key drivers behind the move towards a graduate-led early years profession, of which the creation of EYPS was one aspect.

In line with many other areas of leadership, distributed leadership has received increasing attention in early education in recent years.[13] This has a particular resonance in a sector where many practitioners develop a strong identity as professionals skilled in engaging with children, while exhibiting some resistance to developing their role as leaders and facilitators of others.[14] Some have associated this with the highly feminised nature of the early years workforce and early years leaders, who have often been regarded as mistrusting the whole notion of leadership and its associations with the 'heroic' wielding of power, rather than with nurturing others.[15] In our focus on practice leadership, we drew heavily on findings from teacher leadership research (Hartley, 2007)[16] which are based on a similar workforce and emphasise the importance of relationships between practitioners and the shared and distributed nature of this form of leadership.

Our research into practice leadership represents, at one level, an attempt to apply a less contentious, and more contextually appropriate, notion of leadership to the context of early education. Before exploring the literature on early years leadership and its links to the notion of quality improvement, it is important to outline relevant aspects of the changing landscape of early years provision in England over the last 17 years.

Changes in the nature of early years provision in England 1997–2014

Early years provision in England has been subject to an avalanche of change in recent years. Therefore, it is important to preface our exploration of the literature relating to early years leaders and leadership by presenting an overview of the increasingly complex and diverse landscape of early years provision in England. The diversity and recurring challenges that persist in the system stem in part from long-established structures which policy initiatives have found difficult to overcome.

We have taken 1997 as our starting point because the number of early years initiatives introduced in England increased rapidly after the election of the Labour government that year. At that time, many children aged three to five in England did not attend pre-schools and started reception in school in the term of their fifth birthday. Pre-school provision comprised nursery classes and nursery schools, led by qualified teachers; day nurseries, led by social care staff; private nurseries, led by owners from a variety of backgrounds; and pre-school playgroups, managed by voluntary groups and families, all of which were regulated by local authorities.[17] There was no expectation that staff leaders in non-school provision would be graduates and Level 2 was regarded as a minimum qualification for practitioners.[18] This situation had arisen during a period when the state had consistently avoided committing additional resources to early education places and more mothers stayed at home to care for their children. Voluntary groups had evolved to meet the needs of families who wanted a social educational opportunity for their children and private day care had evolved to meet the needs of professional working parents. The preceding Conservative administration had introduced vouchers as a way of encouraging the market to share the financial burden of pre-school education and empower families to have greater say in increasing provision. Although provision expanded after Labour came to power in 1997, the public–private mix and the funding gap persisted, leaving pre-schools unable to match the salary levels of primary education. The Nutbrown review of early education and childcare qualifications highlighted this gap and the political nature of the issue.[19]

Pressures on single parents and families meant that more parents were seeking childcare and policy makers became increasingly aware of the benefits of using childcare and early education as a strategy for reducing poverty and welfare costs by facilitating parents' working. The EPPE study, commissioned in early 1997 by the Conservative government, reported throughout the next decade and more on the impact of pre-school provision on children in a variety of contexts across England.[20] The study, which increasingly came to influence Labour's early years policy, sampled 141 settings, including a number of flagship integrated centres which provided nursery classes, care and other family services. It followed the progress of 3,000 children in these settings and as they moved into schools. From the outset, the study collected information about children's home backgrounds and used it to analyse the value added by settings at each stage of their education. EPPE's assertion that pre-school had a positive impact on children's attainment at school was used to support the offer of universal provision of pre-school places to all three-year-olds. The study's association of high quality provision with a highly qualified workforce was key to raising expectations that a Level 3 qualification would be set as a minimum for all leaders and establishing the aspiration to move towards a graduate-led workforce. The EPPE study also influenced the implementation of the Early Years Foundation Stage (EYFS),[21] which advocated a more even balance between adult-led and child-led activity in settings. It also emphasised the value of adults engaging in sustained shared thinking in play and adult-led learning, which in turn was reflected in the EYPS standards.[22]

During this period, the government also embarked on a highly ambitious attempt to integrate early childhood education and care services with multi-agency professional working.[23] The clearest symbol of this was the Every Child Matters agenda, which established five outcomes for all children to be achieved with the support of integrated children's services, formalised in the 2004 Children Act.[24] This was followed by The Children's Workforce Strategy, the Childcare Act – which set out a ten-year childcare strategy – and a series of policy documents such as The Children's Plan and Building Brighter Futures, which set out a vision for children's services and the early years workforce, including the introduction of EYPS.[25] As Aubrey et al. (2013) emphasised, all this change created a challenge for developing leaders who could run children's services and early years settings effectively and increase the quality of provision.[26]

The EPPE study's identification of the importance of the home learning environment on children's subsequent learning and achievement led to increased attention being paid to parents' involvement in pre-school education, which was found to be more influential than pre-school and school effects.[27] As a result, working with parents was incorporated alongside core elements of practice leadership, such as promoting effective interaction between staff and children, into the EYPS standards and retained in the Coalition government's policy after 2010. EYPS represented a push from government to encourage the development of a graduate workforce and endorse leaders who met a set of standards closely related to EPPE-based indicators of quality. It was seen as setting a 'gold standard' for early years practitioners,[28] and as part of creating a vision of what was described as 'a world class children's workforce'.[29] EYPS was explicitly targeted at leaders and potential leaders in the private and voluntary sector as a status that would increase quality without introducing a requirement for prohibitively expensive teacher leaders in settings. The question of the equivalence (or not) of EYPS with qualified teacher status has remained a contentious issue.[30] The introduction of EYPS also required leaders to reflect on key quality indicators and their role in influencing staff to meet them. Early Years Professionals had to demonstrate experience and understanding across the whole 0–5 age range, which encouraged many senior practitioners to work with children under three for the first time.

By the time the Coalition government came to power in 2010, the early years sector had been transformed. Most four-year-olds were in nursery, reception or foundation stage classes, with nearly all three-year-olds taking up some sort of pre-school place. The majority of three-year-olds were also taking up places offered by a greatly increased number of childcare providers, which were more evenly spread over the three sectors and intended to form part of an aligned foundation stage covering the whole 0–5 age range. According to Tickell (2011), 103,000 providers were offering 2,442,100 early learning and care places in 2009 (see Table 1.1 for a breakdown of this total).

Table 1.1 Breakdown of provision across the early years sector in 2011

Type	No. of providers
Full day care (including children's centres)	4,100
Sessional providers (including day care for less than 4 hours in any one day in non-domestic premises)	7,800
After-school clubs	7,900
Holiday clubs	6,400
Childminders	51,000
Nursery schools	450
Primary schools with nursery and reception classes	6,700
Primary schools with reception but no nursery classes	8,600

Source: Tickell (2011)

Other key early years policies introduced by the Coalition included increasing funding for provision for children aged under two and commissioning a review of early education and childcare qualifications (Nutbrown, 2012). This underlined the continuing need to improve training and professional development routes for the early years workforce. While critical of initial levels of training, the report noted the improved quality associated with higher education training in the Graduate Leader Fund evaluation and the increases in confidence reported in the first national survey of Early Years Practitioners (EYPs).[31] Nutbrown also advocated the continued development of setting leaders towards Qualified Teacher Status, alongside increased focus on supporting less experienced practitioners. The government's decision to replace EYPS with the Early Years Teacher (EYT) role in 2013, which still retained many elements of the EYPS standards, was in part a response to Nutbrown and to the recommendation to improve the progression structure for early year qualifications in the review of EYFS.[32] However, there was still no undertaking to move towards pay parity with qualified teacher status. As a result, many children continued to attend private and voluntary settings which are unable to offer qualified teacher level salaries. Indeed, early years provision managed by local authorities continues to be under pressure to reduce staffing costs and be financially viable to a far greater extent than schools are. Consequently, settings have had limited scope to increase their fees and, together with low levels of government subsidy, this has disincentivised practitioners from becoming EYTs, reducing its potential as a mechanism for driving quality improvement in the sector. At the same time, the enduring willingness of a predominantly female workforce to work long hours with low pay continues to characterise the sector and act as a barrier to change.[33]

Early Years Professional Status (EYPS)

This book uses detailed research into practitioners with EYPS to explore and develop the idea of practice leadership that it helped introduce to early years provision. Therefore, before examining early years leadership, it is important to outline EYPS in more detail.

EYPS was launched in 2007 and originally heralded in the DfES's *Children's Workforce Strategy*, which was committed to:

> The establishment of a standard for the professional skills, knowledge and practice experience to be required of someone taking a co-ordinating role will help bring coherence and structure to workforce development across the early years, and will dovetail with the development of the integrated qualifications framework. It will articulate a clear ambition for career progression routes which enable the sector to 'grow its own' professionals.
>
> (DfES, 2006b: 30)[34]

EYPS was part of a range of measures to develop a more professional early years workforce that would raise the status of working with pre-school children. It was also linked to other quality improvement efforts in the sector, such as the implementation of the EYFS,[35] which featured strongly in the first of the 39 standards in the original EYPS framework:

> Candidates for Early Years Professional Status must demonstrate through their practice that a secure knowledge and understanding of the following underpins their own practice and informs their leadership of others.
>
> **S1** The principles and content of the Early Years Foundation Stage and how to put them in to practice.
>
> (CWDC, 2010: 99)[36]

As has already been indicated, EYPS developed out of a growing awareness of the link between practitioners' levels of qualification and the quality of provision that had been highlighted in the EPPE study.[37] Together with the ELEYS[38] and REPEY[39] studies, EPPE identified particular settings where leadership appeared to enhance later outcomes for children and the ELEYS findings in particular were reflected in the emphasis on the importance of leading practice and leadership for learning in the EYPS standards.[40]

At the time of the EPPE study there were relatively low numbers of graduate leaders in the sector as a whole, particularly in the private, voluntary and independent (PVI) settings that formed the majority of the provision. Additionally, there was limited coverage of child development and care routines for the under-fives in teacher training in England. This situation contrasted sharply with the training of the workforce in countries such as Denmark and New Zealand.[41] The government's ambitious target, later dropped by the Coalition government, was for every children's centre to have an EYP by 2010 and for other settings to have an EYP by 2015. Settings in disadvantaged areas were to have two EYPs. EYPS was also seen as important in challenging EYPs' perceived lack of status, associated with the longstanding cultural division between nurseries led by early education professionals and those led by care professionals. The development of EYPS was in part an attempt to integrate these perspectives and to shake off the wider perception of EYPs as being primarily unskilled carers.[42]

Candidates for EYPS were required to meet 39 predetermined standards (simplified to 31 in 2012). They covered areas such as effective practice, teamwork and collaboration, and professional development, with EYPs adopting a leadership role throughout their setting(s). In the original EYPS standards their leadership role was defined as:

> catalysts for change and innovation: they are key to raising the quality of Early Years provision and they exercise leadership in making a positive difference to children's wellbeing, learning and development.
> (CWDC, 2010: 17)

Beyond linking EYP leadership to improvements in quality and outcomes, the standards recognised that, in practice, what this entails will vary from setting to setting, depending on local circumstances. They were explicitly described as 'change agents to improve practice',[43] influencing and inspiring their colleagues and exemplifying high standards of practice. However, ambiguity remained in relation to EYPs' position in a setting or group of settings and how they were to effect what Murray refers to as 'transformational leadership activity'.[44] This lack of clarity is also reflected in the research literature: 'As the EYP role develops, it is EYPs themselves who are helping to shape our understanding of leadership'.[45] This has led to a growth in the number of terms used to describe EYP leaders. They have been described as transformational leaders who, as 'change agents', motivate others towards higher goals.[46] Their leadership has been compared also to existing models such as pedagogical leadership and leadership for learning.[47] In part, it was this level of confusion and conflation with other forms of leadership that led us not to conceptualise practice leadership as a distinct style or approach to leadership. Rather, we saw it as a strand of activity in which all leaders in the early years would be 'required' to be involved because of the nature of the external pressures they were under from inspections and new government policies.

Defining quality provision

The next key area of policy and research to address is concerned with defining the quality of provision in the early years. Fenech (2011) described three waves of research into quality and early childhood education and care since the 1970s.[48] The first wave was concerned with evaluating the effects of non-maternal care on child development. The second began to examine how quality was constructed in early childhood provision and is associated with the development of rating scales, such as the Early Childhood Environment Rating Scale (ECERS) and the Infant/Toddler Environment Rating Scale (ITERS), both of which have been revised subsequently.[49] The third wave took a more ecological approach, investigating the effects of children's individual characteristics and families on quality and outcomes.

Notions of quality in effective early years provision have been the focus of much debate in recent years. Mathers et al. (2011) recognised that this was in part because debates encompass research-based measures, professional standards (including inspection frameworks) and the views of stakeholders such as parents, children and providers.[50] These three broad categories are each associated with a range of potential definitions of quality and means of measurement. Furthermore, different notions of quality arise primarily because of the various perspectives of those making judgements and the types of measures and frameworks they use. Perspectives may come from 'insiders', such as practitioners, or 'outsiders', such as inspectors and researchers. They may be 'bottom up', in that they include the views of children and practitioners, or 'top down', from the perspective of owners and funders.[51] Measurements of quality tend to be categorised as either objective, being a single agreed measure of what constitutes quality, or relativist, being derived from a range of criteria that vary depending on the stakeholders involved.

Proponents of the objective approach argue for quality assessments to be based on 'a collection of measurable characteristics in the childcare environment that affect children's social and cognitive development'.[52] More relativist perspectives hold that quality is 'a constructed concept, subjective in nature and based on values, beliefs and interest, rather than an objective and universal reality'.[53] As objective measures allow more scope for comparison between settings, they tend to be favoured by researchers and inspectors, but they are restricted in that they only include what can be measured consistently and reliably. Relativist approaches are founded on more holistic judgements that view quality 'as a subjective, value-based, relative and dynamic concept'.[54] However, although such judgements are more able to capture a wide range of perspectives, they also leave themselves open to criticism for being so specific to individual contexts that they cannot provide general assessments of quality that can be linked to nationally defined standards or outcomes for children.[55]

Reviewing quality in relation to the EPPE study, Sylva (2010) drew attention to Munton and colleagues' preference for combining different quality indicators, instead of relying on individuals' judgements of quality.[56] As Sylva notes, measuring outcomes is complex and necessitates longitudinal research to investigate the progress and achievement of children in a number of settings:

> *Using objective, measurable definitions of quality has produced a wealth of research showing a clear relationship between the quality of early childhood provision and children's developmental outcomes.*

> (Sylva, 2010: 71)

This is important because it highlights the relationship between three key dimensions of quality: structures (facilities and human resources), processes (the everyday educational and care experiences of children) and output measures (outcomes for children). In our research, this distinction was used to understand the relationship between practice leaders' impact on key input measures and the likely effect this would have on later outcomes for children. Our methodology, therefore, was based on objective assessments of the quality of settings' processes and input quality and the role that practice leaders played in improving these over time. We then used the EPPE findings[57] to identify which of these input measures would be most likely to result in improved, long-term outcomes for children.

Studying and conceptualising leadership in the early years

As we began by stating, research into early years leadership has proliferated in recent years, particularly when it has been concerned with identifying the forms of effective leadership that have been associated with achieving improvement in settings.[58] As the emerging evidence base, both in the UK and internationally, has begun to explore the links between leadership and improved provision, it has begun to focus on those aspects that have been seen as having the most direct impact on the practice of others, hence the emphasis on notions such as 'practice leader' and 'change agent'.[59] The policy focus on effective early years leadership has led to the expectation that they will lead practice across a range of pedagogical areas: Hallet and Roberts-Holmes (2010) described them as 'leaders of learning'.[60] Recent research has explored EYPs' dual role of leading practice and acting as change agents in early years settings.[61] Heikka and Waniganayake suggested that the study of leadership in early childhood education should be informed by approaches that are sensitive to the ways in which leaders develop others' leadership by distributing responsibilities. They related leading practice to the concept of pedagogical leadership, which they define as:

> taking responsibility for the shared understanding of the aims and methods of learning and teaching of young children from birth to 8 years. In these discussions, teachers have a significant role and responsibility to ensure that the educational pedagogy employed matches children's interests, abilities and needs.
>
> (Heikka and Waniganayake, 2011: 500)

They also made a strong case for more rigorous research into pedagogical leadership in early childhood settings, arguing that early childhood leadership involves combining both pedagogical and distributed forms of leadership, as leaders are responsible for creating a community that fosters learning and communication. They assert that, in practice, pedagogical leadership 'has to be considered within the full extent of leadership roles and responsibilities expected of today's early childhood leaders'.[62] These findings resonate with outcomes from the ELEYS study suggesting that 'distributed', 'participative', 'facilitative' or 'collaborative' models of leadership are effective in early years settings.[63]

Effectiveness research in leadership places a great deal of emphasis on the 'causal chain' that links leaders' activities, their influence on the practice of others, and overall improvements in the quality of provision. In focusing on how these links hold together, it is important not to oversimplify how they are formed in the first instance. We examine this in depth in Chapter 2. Before that, however, it is important to look in detail at the role played by professional identity and the interplay of formal and informal leadership roles.

Professional identity and change agency

In this section, we try to unpack some of the inherent complexity in trying to link the activities of individual leaders to outcomes for children. The first area we want to problematise is the relationship between professional identity and agency. As we discuss in Chapter 2, we treat this as the link between what people think they should be doing as leaders, shaped by their sense of professional identity, and what they think they can achieve, their professional agency. Discussing agency and identity means considering the nature and impact of the structures that surround leaders. The next link is between individual and collective agency, which in this instance is discussed with reference to the interactions between the formal and informal leadership structures in settings.

The formal leaders of a setting have a number of structures they can use to influence the practice of others, from rescheduling the timetable or rejigging the formal leadership arrangements to changing role descriptions and pay scales. The efficacy of purely structural changes as a means of improving practice has been consistently called into doubt across a number of phases of change theory. Summed up in the phrase 'don't just re-structure, re-culture' is the notion that changing the norms and beliefs of those in a setting is a necessary part of effective change management. In the era of the 'change agent', structural changes were seen as less important than empower-ing individuals to take responsibility for the changes in which they were involved. However, this focus on the agency of the individuals had two unfortunate outcomes: it underplayed the importance of certain forms of structure on shaping the agency of individuals and failed to recognise the importance of collective agency, the capacity of practitioners in a setting to work collaboratively. More recently, these shortcomings have begun to be addressed.

The focus on individuals as change agents highlighted the impact of certain 'deep structures' on their agency.[64] These deep structures range from professional beliefs about children and learning to social and cognitive constructs such as 'trust'. The recognition that such deep structures shape what people believe they can do, as well as what they should do, has brought the notion of professional identity to the fore in both leadership and change management research.[65] This is because professional identity is a broad construct covering a range of these structures, including the multiple aspects of individuals' sense of self and how these are constructed in part by others. The importance of self-perception and confidence is frequently discussed in leadership literature.[66] Identity formation, particularly in relation to profes-sional identity, has a strong social element and, as Miller and Cable (2011) have discussed, increased expectations of early education and care have had an impact on early years leaders' sense of professionalism. As we have emphasised, the move towards leaders in the sector being graduates, in which EYPS was a central policy, was intended to improve the professional status of such leaders. As Hevey noted, this was done at speed:

> The early years sector was being asked to undergo transformation from largely unqualified to graduate level leadership in less than 10 years – a process that has taken other professions more than 50 years to achieve.
>
> (Hevey, 2010: 161)[67]

This may account for the concerns raised by McGillivray (2011) about the limited presence of early years leaders' voices in this new leadership discourse.[68]

Professional identities shift not only because of changes to the discourses surrounding leadership but also because of individuals' maturation as leaders. In our own research, we discuss this in terms of a three-stage model of 'becoming', 'being' and 'developing' as a practice leader, introduced in Chapter 3. Progression through these stages was closely linked to a practice leader's sense of agency, particularly in relation to the extent to which they could effect change by building capacity among colleagues. This takes us on to the second area to discuss, the links between individual and collective agency.

The importance of building collective understanding and commitment to shared goals and aims is a key part of effective leadership. Establishing a sense of community, developing respect, valuing colleagues and embracing diversity have all been found to be key in developing participative and inclusive notions of leadership.[69] The effectiveness of these strategies lies in their ability to develop and enhance the collective agency of those in a setting. Discussions about generating this kind of collective agency from a leadership perspective tend to draw on theories of distributed leadership such as have been proposed by Spillane et al. (2004) and Harris (2004),[70] while in organisational terms they are more likely to be related to building capacity for improvement.[71]

There has been growing interest in the application of distributed leadership to early education in recent years,[72] although, as with its application in school contexts, the rhetoric surrounding it has often moved ahead of the evidence. Muijs et al. (2004) and Aubrey (2011) endorsed distributed leadership as having considerable potential application amidst the diversity and complexity of the early years sector, although more recent research has emphasised the importance of applying multiple leadership models flexibly.[73] We introduce the notion of distributed leadership at this point because it also highlights the importance of interactions between formal and informal patterns of leadership such as those described by Spillane et al. (2004).[74]

It is important to distinguish between formal and informal leadership in order to understand different interpretations of what constitutes distributed leadership and what is meant when leadership is discussed as a social rather than an individual phenomenon. A formal leader's influence is seen as depending in part on their position in a leadership hierarchy, while the influence of informal leaders is mainly derived from their standing in the professional networks that exist in and around settings.[75] Approaches to distributed leadership can in part be distinguished by the extent to which formal leaders legitimate or incorporate these informal networks into formal structures, or adapt these structures to exploit them.

The idea of distributing leadership highlights the importance of collective agency because it emphasises the fact that leadership occurs in a social context coloured by interrelationships among practitioners. It is 'stretched over the work of a number of individuals and the task is accomplished through the interaction of multiple leaders'.[76] Despite (or perhaps because of) this level of interest in it, distributed leadership has increasingly attracted criticism, notably for lacking evidence of its effectiveness in improving teaching and learning and for ignoring the micro-political elements of leadership practice.[77] However, the association of its rise with such policy initiatives as extended school provision and inter-agency working and the notion that the 'heterarchy' of distributed leadership resides uneasily within the formal bureaucracy of schools[78] suggest that it may have a more secure place in the more collaborative and fluid context of early years settings. Hard and Jónsdóttir (2013), for example, claim that concerns about the dangers of delegating responsibility to under-qualified and inexperienced staff may be overcome by skilful leaders, underlining the fact that collaboration depends on effective leadership.[79] Heikka et al. (2013) suggest that the diversity of early years settings, which often incorporate a range of programmes and staff from varying backgrounds, lends itself to distributed leadership research's focus on the 'intersection of diverse stakeholders, situations and structures'.[80] However, it should be noted that more empirically based research found that developed forms of distributed leadership were rare in the early years sector being studied.[81]

All of this suggests that, applied judiciously, more social definitions of leadership, such as distributed leadership, have much to offer the study of early years leadership. In fact, leadership in the early years may well resemble the kind of 'hybrid leadership' that Gronn has promoted in recent writing to overcome what he saw as the polarity between focused and distributed notions of leadership to promote the 'intermingling of both hierarchical and heterarchical modes of ordering responsibilities and relations'.[82] His image of configurations or constellations of leadership allowing for a greater flow of interactions in leadership activity, with his concept of 'conjoint agency expressed in concertive actions',[83] offers a somewhat different take on the nature of collective agency. This notion of hybrid leadership, combined with elements of distributed leadership perspectives and the strong evidence base relating to teacher leadership, guided our examination of practice leadership in action in Chapters 4 and 5. Our approach is based on detailed case studies of *enacted* leadership in early years settings, informed by evidence from the broader field of educational research, which has often seemed to be lacking in the early education context.[84]

Summary: studying practice leadership in relation to improving the quality of settings

This brief discussion of professional identity and collective agency indicates the shortcomings of any study that tries simplistically to link leaders' actions with later outcomes for children. There are potentially numerous factors that shape what leaders do, from their own professional understandings and the contextual pressures they face in their settings to the wider professional discourses that surround them. We discuss our approach to researching within this complexity in Chapter 2, where we describe how we based our approach on combining an objective measure of quality, which allowed for comparative analyses across settings with very different characteristics, with a broad framework for generating an in-depth understanding of how leaders adapted their approaches to the contexts in which they operated.

Rather than seeking to categorise all the different styles and configurations of leadership that we encountered in the study, this framework allowed us to look at how these leaders constructed their notion of practice leadership, what activities they included in this strand of their work, and if and how they developed collective agency in their settings. Our overall aim for this book was not to generate a new general theory of leadership or to map the prevalence of different leadership styles, but rather to discuss the 'how' of leadership. How did these leaders set about their task of trying to improve the quality of their provision? How successful were they in their efforts, as measured by the models of quality we used? We set out to try and answer these questions to help practitioners with another question: 'How should I set out to improve practice in my setting?'

Notes

1   See, for example, Fenech, M. (2011) An analysis of the conceptualisation of 'quality' in early childhood education and care empirical research: promoting 'blind spots' as foci for future research, *Contemporary Issues in Early Childhood*, 12 (2), 102–17; Mathers, S., Ranns, H., Karemaker, A.M., Moody, A., Sylva, K., Graham, J. and Siraj-Blatchford, I. (2011) *Evaluation of Graduate Leader Fund: Final Report*. London: DfE.

2   Siraj-Blatchford, I. and Manni, L. (2007) *Effective Leadership in the Early Years Sector*. London: Institute of Education, University of London; Ofsted (2008) *Early Years: Leading to Excellence*. London: Ofsted.

3   Teaching Agency (2012a) *Review of the Early Years Professional Status Standards*. London: Teaching Agency.

4   See Muijs, D., Aubrey, C., Harris, A. and Briggs, M. (2004) How do they manage? A review of the research on leadership in early childhood, *Journal of Early Childhood Research*, 2 (2), 157–69; Aubrey, C., Godfrey, R. and Harris, A. (2013) How do they manage? An investigation of early childhood leadership, *Educational Management Administration and Leadership*, 41 (5), 5–29.

5   Aubrey, C. (2011) *Leading and Managing in the Early Years*, 2nd edn. London: Sage; Balkundi, P. and Harrison, D.A. (2006) Ties, leaders, and time in teams:

strong inference about the effects of network structure on team viability and performance, *Academy of Management Journal*, 49, 49–68.

6   Rodd, J. (2006) *Leadership in Early Childhood: The Pathway to Professionalism*. Buckingham: Open University Press.

7   Aubrey (2011).

8   Moyles, J. (2006) *Effective Leadership and Management in the Early Years*. Maidenhead: Open University Press.

9   Aubrey (2011).

10 Anning, A., Cottrell, D., Frost, N., Green, J. and Robinson, M. (2006) *Developing Multiprofessional Teamwork for Integrated Children's Services: Research, policy and practice*. Maidenhead: Open University Press; Anning, A., Cullen, J. and Fleer, M. (2009) *Early Childhood Education: Society and culture*, 2nd edn. London: Sage.

11 Sylva, K., Melhuish, E., Sammons, P., Siraj-Blatchford, I. and Taggart, B. (2004) *The Final Report: Effective Pre-School Education*. Technical Paper 12: The Effective Provision of Pre-School Education (EPPE Project). London: Institute of Education, University of London/DfES.

12 Siraj-Blatchford and Manni (2007).

13 See, for example, Heikka, J. and Hujala, E. (2013) Early childhood leadership through the lens of distributed leadership, *European Early Childhood Education Research Journal*, 21 (4), 568–80; Heikka, J., Waniganayake, M. and Hujala, E. (2013) Contextualizing distributed leadership within early childhood education: current understandings, research evidence and future challenges, *Educational Management Administration and Leadership*, 41 (1), 30–44.

14 Rodd (2006).

15 See, for example, Moyles (2006); Hard, L. and Jónsdóttir, A.H. (2013) Leadership is not a dirty word: exploring and embracing leadership in ECEC, *European Early Childhood Education Research Journal*, 21 (3), 311–25.

16 Hartley, D. (2007) The emergence of distributed leadership in education: why now?, *British Journal of Educational Studies*, 55 (2), 202–14.

17 See Tickell, C. (2011) *The Early Years: Foundations for Life, Health and Learning. An Independent Report on the Early Years Foundation Stage by Her Majesty's Government*. London: National Archives.

18 Nutbrown, C. (2012) *Foundations for Quality: The Independent Review of Early Education and Childcare Qualifications. Final Report*. London: DfE.

19 Ibid.

20 Sylva, K., Melhuish, E., Sammons, P., Siraj-Blatchford, I. and Taggart, B. (2010) *Early Childhood Matters: Evidence from the Effective Pre-school and Primary Education* Project. London: Routledge.

21 Department for Education and Skills (DfES) (2007) *The Early Years Foundation Stage: Setting the Standards for Learning, Development and Care*. Nottingham: DfES.

22 For the value of shared thinking, see Siraj-Blatchford, I. and Sylva, K. (2004) Researching pedagogy in English pre-schools, *British Educational Research Journal*, 30 (5), 713–30. For the relationship to EYPS standards, see Children's Workforce Development Council (CWDC) (2010) *On the Right Track: Guidance to the Standards for the Award of Early Years Professional Status*. Leeds: CWDC; and Teaching Agency (2012b) *Early Years Professional Status Standards (from September 2012)*. London: Teaching Agency.

23 Roberts-Holmes, G. (2013) The English Early Years Professional Status (EYPS) and the 'split' Early Childhood Education and Care (ECEC) system, *European Early Childhood Education Research Journal*, 21 (3), 339–52.

24 Department for Education and Skills (DfES) (2004) *Children Act*. London: DfES.

25 Department for Education and Skills (DfES) (2005) *Children's Workforce Strategy: A Strategy to Build a World-class Workforce for Children and Young People*. London: DfES; Department for Education and Skills (DfES) (2006a) *Childcare Act*. London: DfES; Department for Education and Skills (DfES) (2006b) *Children's Workforce Strategy: Building a World-class Workforce for Children, Young People and Families – The Government's Response to the Consultation*. London: DfES; Department for Children, Schools and Families (DCSF) (2007) *The Children's Act: Building Brighter Futures*. London: DCSF; Department for Children, Schools and Families (DCSF) (2008) *Building Brighter Futures: Next Steps for the Children's Workforce*. London: DCSF.

26 Aubrey et al. (2013).

27 Sylva et al. (2010).

28 Children's Workforce Development Council (CWDC) (2008) *Early Years Professional Status*. Leeds: CWDC.

29 DfES (2005), at p. 3.

30 Roberts-Holmes (2013).

31 See Mathers et al. (2011) and Hadfield, M., Jopling, M., Royle, K. and Waller, T. (2011) *First National Survey of Practitioners with Early Years Professional Status*. London: CWDC, respectively.

32 Tickell (2011).

33 Miller, M. and Cable, C. (eds.) (2011) *Professionalization, Leadership and Management in the Early Years*. London: Sage.

34 DfES (2006b).

35 DCSF (2008).

36 Ibid.

37 Sylva et al. (2004).

38 Siraj-Blatchford and Manni (2007).

39 Sylva et al. (2010).

40 CWDC (2010).

41 The situation in those countries is described by Nurse, A. (2007) *The New Early Years Professionals*. London: Routledge; Miller, M. and Cable, C. (eds.)

(2008) *Professionalism in the Early Years Workforce*. London: Hodder; Mooney, A., Cameron, C., Candappa, M., McQuail, S., Moss, P. and Petrie, P. (2003) *Early Years and Childcare International Evidence Project: Quality*. London: DfES.

42   Lloyd, E. and Hallet, E. (2010) Professionalising the early childhood workforce in England: work in progress or missed opportunity?, *Contemporary Issues in Early Childhood*, 11 (1), 75–86.

43   Children's Workforce Development Council (CWDC) (2006) *Early Years Professional Status Prospectus*. Leeds: CWDC.

44   See Whalley, M. (2011) Leading and managing in the early years, in L. Miller and C. Cable (eds.) *Professionalization, Leadership and Management in the Early Years*. London: Sage; Murray, J. (2013) Becoming an early years professional: developing a new professional identity, *European Early Childhood Education Research Journal*, 21 (4), 527–40, at p. 538; Roberts-Holmes (2013).

45   Whalley (2011), at p. 4.

46   Miller and Cable (2011), at p. 16.

47   See Heikka, J. and Waniganayake, M. (2011) Pedagogical leadership from a distributed perspective within the context of early childhood education, *International Journal of Leadership in Education: Theory and Practice*, 14 (4), 499–512 and Siraj-Blatchford and Manni (2007), respectively.

48   Fenech (2011).

49   Harms, T., Clifford, R. and Cryer, D. (1998) *Early Childhood Environment Rating Scale* (revised edn.). New York, NY: Teachers College Press; Harms, T., Cryer, D. and Clifford, R.M. (2003) *Infant/Toddler Environment Rating Scale – Revised*. New York, NY: Teachers College Press.

50   Mathers et al. (2011).

51   Katz, L.G. (1995) *Talks with Teachers of Young Children: A Collection*. Norwood, NJ: Ablex.

52   Siraj-Blatchford, I. and Wong, Y. (1999) Defining and evaluating quality in early childhood education in an international context: dilemmas and possibilities, *Early Years: An International Journal of Research and Development*, 20 (1), 7–18, at p. 10.

53   Moss, P. and Pence, A. (eds.) (1994) *Valuing Quality in Early Childhood Services: New Approaches to Defining Quality*. London: Paul Chapman, at p. 172.

54   Dahlberg, G. and Moss, P. (2008) Beyond quality in early childhood education and care – languages of evaluation, *New Zealand Journal of Teachers' Work*, 5 (1), 3–12, at p. 5.

55   Mathers et al. (2011).

56   Munton, A.G., Mooney, A. and Rowland, L. (1995) Deconstructing quality: a conceptual framework for the new paradigm in day care provision for the under eights, *Early Childhood Development and Care*, 114, 11–23.

57   Sylva et al. (2004).

58   Ofsted (2008).

59 Whalley, M. (2008) *Leading Practice in Early Years Settings (Achieving EYPS)*. Exeter: Learning Matters.

60 Hallet, E. and Roberts-Holmes, G. (2010) *The contribution of the Early Years Professional Status role to quality improvement strategies in Gloucestershire: Final Report*. Unpublished Manuscript, Institute of Education, University of London.

61 See, for example, Heikka and Waniganayake (2011); Davis, G. and Barry, A. (2013) Positive outcomes for children: early years professionals effecting change, *Early Child Development and Care*, 183 (1), 37–48.

62 Heikka and Waniganayake (2011), at p. 499.

63 Siraj-Blatchford and Manni (2007), at p. 19.

64 See Giddens, A. (1984) *The Constitution of Society: Outline of the Theory of Structuration*. Berkeley, CA: University of California Press; Wellman, B. and Berkowitz, S. (eds.) (1988) *Social Structures: A Network Approach*. New York, NY: Cambridge University Press.

65 See Geijsel, F. and Meijers, F. (2005) Identity learning: the core process of educational change, *Educational Studies*, 31 (4), 419–30; Pyhalto, K., Pietarinen, J. and Soini, T. (2014) Comprehensive school teachers' professional agency in large-scale educational change, *Journal of Educational Change*, 15 (3), 303–25.

66 See, for example, Rodd (2006); Jones, C. and Pound, L. (2008) *Leadership and Management in the Early Years*. Maidenhead: Open University Press; Miller and Cable (2011).

67 Hevey, D. (2010) Developing a new profession: a case study, *Literacy Information and Computer Education Journal*, 1 (3), 159–67.

68 McGillivray, G. (2011) Constructions of professional identity, in L. Miller and C. Cable (eds.) *Professionalization, Leadership and Management in the Early Years*. London: Sage.

69 Rodd (2006); Siraj-Blatchford and Manni (2007); and Murray (2013).

70 Spillane, J., Halverson, R. and Diamond, J. (2004) Towards a theory of leadership practice: a distributed perspective, *Journal of Curriculum Studies*, 36 (1), 3–34; Harris, A. (2004) Distributed leadership and school improvement: leading or misleading?, *Educational Management and Administration*, 32 (1), 11–24.

71 See Buono, A.F. and Kerber, K.W. (2008) The challenge of organizational change: enhancing organizational change capacity, *Revue Sciences de Gestion*, 65, 99–118.

72 See Aubrey (2011); Heikka and Hujala (2013); Heikka et al. (2013).

73 See Aubrey et al. (2013).

74 Spillane et al. (2004).

75 Hard, L. (2004) How is leadership understood in early childhood education and care?, *Journal of Australian Research in Early Childhood Education*, 11 (1), 123–31.

76 Spillane, J.P., Halverson, R. and Diamond, J.B. (2001) Investigating school leadership practice, *Educational Researcher*, 30 (3), 23–8.
77 Robinson, V.M. (2008) Forging the links between distributed leadership and educational outcomes, *Journal of Educational Administration*, 46 (2), 241–56; Hatcher, R. (2005) The distribution of leadership and power in schools, *British Journal of Sociology of Education*, 26 (2), 253–67.
78 Hartley, D. (2009) Paradigms: how far does research in distributed leadership 'stretch'?, *Educational Management Administration and Leadership*, 38 (3), 271–85.
79 Hard and Jónsdóttir (2013).
80 Heikka et al. (2013), at p. 40.
81 Heikka and Hujala (2013).
82 Gronn, P. (2008) The future of distributed leadership, *Journal of Educational Administration*, 46 (2), 141–58 and Gronn, P. (2011) Hybrid configurations of leadership, in A. Bryman, D. Collinson, K. Grint, B. Jackson and M. Uhl-Bien (eds.) *Sage Handbook of Leadership*. London: Sage. The quotation is from Gronn (2008), at p. 150.
83 Gronn (2008); Gronn, P. (2002) Distributed leadership as a unit of analysis, *Leadership Quarterly*, 13 (4), 423–51. The quotation is from Gronn (2008), at p. 150.
84 Aubrey et al. (2013).

2   Practice leadership

Our focus on practice leadership started as a way of defining what was distinct about a group of early years practitioners we were researching on behalf of the UK government. These professionals had been described as 'practice leaders' and were being supported to take on the challenge of improving the quality of provision in their settings. Researching, and reflecting on, what these professionals saw as practice leadership helped us to assess their impact on the quality of the settings in which they were working. As we applied the idea of practice leadership to a range of settings and leaders, we began to conceptualise it as a way of studying leadership more generally in the early years. In this chapter, we outline some of the thought processes and conceptual developments we went through as we applied the notion of practice leadership to explore leaders' activities in early years settings where they focused on improving the quality of settings' provision. The arguments in this chapter set the scene for the later descriptions of how effective practice transformed the quality of settings' provision.

Background

The EYPS practitioners we were researching were expected to engage in 'practice leadership'[1] and 'exercise leadership in making a positive difference to children's wellbeing, learning and development'.[2] The overall aim of our research was to assess the impact of these practice leaders on the settings in which they worked, in order to understand how they attempted to bring about improvements in the quality of provision in these settings.

At the heart of our research agenda were two deceptively simple research questions: 'What impact were these practitioners having on the quality of provision?' and 'How were they able to bring about improvements in quality?' After reviewing the existing literature and beginning our research into what these practice leaders were involved in to improve the quality of provision, we began to treat practice leadership as a strand of activity in which most early years leaders were engaged in some way. Practice leadership is not a new style or form of leadership; rather, it is a lens through which to view the links between the actions of leaders, both those in formal leadership positions and informal leaders, and improvements to the quality of provision. As a lens it focuses on how leaders try to bring about improvements, both to enhancde their settings' capacity for change and in response to the challenges they face.

As we began our research, we developed the concept of practice leadership partly as our response to previous critiques of early years leadership research and partly as a methodological innovation. As outlined in Chapter 1, the literature exploring leadership in the early years had frequently critiqued its failure comprehensively to encapsulate the highly contextualised and dynamic nature of leadership. We were about to begin research in 30 early years settings, following over 40 practitioners with EYPS for three years. These practitioners held different leadership positions and worked in a diverse range of settings, in terms of the quality of provision and the communities they served. Much of the existing literature had limited applicability to such a broad range of contexts. With one or two notable exceptions, there was also a lack of data concerning the impact of leadership on outcomes for children. A key critique of the existing literature on leadership in the early years echoes that of those working in the school sector,[3] namely that it has failed sufficiently to highlight the role played by context and has provided little evidence of how leaders bring about effective change. This critique was based on the argument that focusing on defining effective leaders' 'traits' and 'characteristics' had led to models that were at best too general and at worst banal. We hoped that focusing on one strand of leadership activity would help us to answer this critique by capturing the 'situational' nature of early years leadership and reflecting the 'contextual literacy' of its leaders.[4]

Studying the impact of around 43 'practice leaders' across 30 settings for three years required not only the development of an innovative conceptual framework, but also some methodological ingenuity. (The numbers of practitioners with EYPS in the case study settings varied during the research owing to typical turnover patterns.) Randomised control trials or matched sample designs were inappropriate, in part because previous research had already shown that gaining EYPS had a positive effect on the quality of provision,[5] but also because of the technical difficulties of randomising or building a representative sample of this population cost-effectively. The funders had asked for a case study sampling framework that covered a range of leaders, at different stages of their careers, working in settings rated by Ofsted from satisfactory to outstanding. As they were most concerned with understanding how these practice leaders affected the quality of provision in their settings over time, we deliberately ensured that settings rated satisfactory by Ofsted were over-represented in the sample in order to determine whether practice leaders could bring about improvement in these more difficult contexts. Therefore, these cases were not going to be retrospective reconstructions of what outstanding leaders claimed to have achieved. Rather, they were to be contemporaneous accounts of how early years leaders succeeded, or failed, in making a significant difference in their settings. The case studies therefore needed to capture, in real time, their leadership practices and aspirations. The notion of practice leadership therefore helped us frame and boundary the case studies and draw cross-case generalisations where appropriate.

How, then, did we start to construct how practice leadership has been interpreted by the leaders in our case studies? Our starting point was another strand of our research – two national surveys of practitioners with EYPS.[6] Just over 3,000 responses were generated by the two surveys, representing around 2,000 different practitioners in all and resulting in a broadly representative sample of approximately 30 per cent of the total population of EYPs at the time. The surveys provided a unique snapshot of these practice leaders' activities.

Practice leadership – roles, duties and workloads

The standards for achieving EYPS developed and evolved over time and varied in their references to leadership roles. The revised standards expressed a clear set of expectations about leading practice:

Lead practice and foster a culture of continuous improvement

- Model and implement effective practice, and support and mentor other practitioners.
- Reflect on the effectiveness of provision, propose appropriate changes and influence, shape and support the implementation of policies and practices within the setting.
- Take responsibility for improving practice through appropriate professional development, for self and colleagues.
- Promote equality of opportunity through championing children's rights and anti-discriminatory practice.
- Understand the implications of relevant legislation, statutory frameworks, including the EYFS, and policy for early years settings and apply in practice.

(Teaching Agency, 2012b)[7]

Although practitioners would need to evidence these standards to obtain EYPS, there were likely to be considerable differences between meeting a set of requirements and the day-to-day realities of leadership. The two national surveys allowed us to build up a picture of the scope and depth of these practitioners' leadership activities.

In general, the data collected from the surveys confirmed the oft-made assertions that early childhood leadership is marked by a multiplicity of roles and that settings vary widely in their make-up and composition.[8] The question we needed to answer was to what extent such variability had resulted in differences in leadership activities. This was a key methodological issue, since in the case studies we had to consider whether we should treat our participants as a single group of leaders or split them into different groups, perhaps categorised by their position in formal leadership structures or by the type of setting in which they worked. We had to ensure that our case study design and our approach to cross-case analysis could accommodate and address such variability.

In the first survey, practitioners were asked to describe their current roles using a number of set categories. These leadership roles were differentiated by degree of responsibility, in part expressed by the role they had played in bringing in the EYFS. They were:

- Owner/manager/deputy – lead/manage/oversee the setting/more than one setting, lead/implement/support in implementing EYFS, team leader/manager
- Senior early years worker – lead practice, lead/manage/oversee/ monitor/support the EYFS, team leader
- Room leader – lead/manage/oversee room, lead/manage/oversee EYFS, lead practitioner, team leader
- Early years worker – lead and/or support staff
- Admin/finance/facility worker – team leader
- Local authority (LA) staff – leading on learning/pedagogy

As Figure 2.1 indicates, the majority of these practice leaders were concentrated in what might be described as senior leadership roles, being owners and managers of settings or their deputies. Nearly one-fifth appeared to be middle leaders, i.e. senior early years workers and room leaders, while another 10 per cent of workers were termed practitioner-leaders.

The second survey unpicked these categories in more detail and revealed that a large proportion (approximately 20 per cent) of all owner/managers were in charge of multiple settings. It also provided more detailed analysis of practitioners working in school settings, as illustrated in Figure 2.2.

In the second survey, the practitioners were also asked to state their key duties in their own words, placing their main duties first. Thematic analysis of

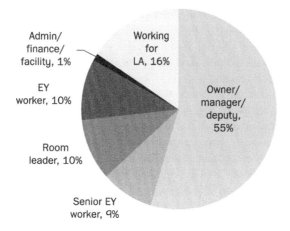

Figure 2.1 Breakdown of roles: national survey 1 (responses = 1,045).

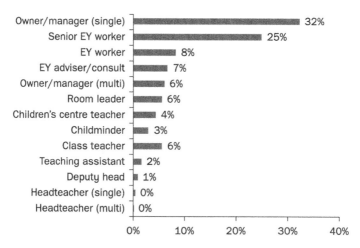

Figure 2.2 Practitioners' roles: national survey 2 (responses = 1,680).

these open responses produced the following results, with the order of the duties reflecting the frequency with which they were cited.

1   Owner/manager/ head/deputy head
    • Lead/manage/oversee the setting/more than one setting
    • Lead/implement/support in implementing EYFS
    • Train/support staff
    • Plan/deliver care and/or education
    • Writing/compliance with policies
    • Work with families

2   Senior early years worker
  • Lead practice
  • Lead/manage/oversee/monitor/support the EYFS
  • Responsible for/oversee care and/or education
  • Supervision of children/staff
  • Developing partnerships
  • Cover manager's absence/liaise with manager
  • Improve/reflect on practice
  • Promote ethos and values
3   Room leader
  • Lead/manage/oversee room
  • Lead/manage/oversee EYFS
  • Provide care and/or education
  • Organise parent groups
  • Plan activities and/or observations
  • Cover manager's absence/liaise closely with manager
  • Manage/coordinate staff
  • Train staff
4   Early years worker
  • Care for/supervise children (also includes child protection officer)
  • Plan and deliver sessions/discuss planning with teachers
  • SEN matters
  • Observation
  • Lead and/or support staff

The significance of this analysis in relation to the case study design and the idea of practice leadership was its identification of the very similar activities being undertaken by individuals in different roles, such as the leadership and management of staff and the planning and delivery of practice. However, there was some evidence that the degree of responsibility for delivering the EYFS varied according to leadership level.

The main differences in leadership activities across the six categories in which the practitioners placed themselves were related more to the scale and scope of the activities than their nature. The scale of the leadership activities ranged from overseeing a single practitioner or being responsible for a single room to managing a group of nurseries. The scope of their leadership activities varied considerably across and within the categories and reflected the extent to which they were leading across different aspects of their setting's (or settings') development. While some of these practice leaders might only be leading on one area of practice, others had remits that spanned almost the complete range of practices in their setting.

We were also able to examine the specifics of different leaders' duties and responsibilities in the second survey. Rather than simply listing their main duties, we asked for a more detailed workload analysis outlining how practitioners spent their time. In order to simplify the analysis, the range of leadership roles used in the first survey was collapsed into three main categories: owner/managers and headteachers were classified as 'senior leaders'; children's centre teachers, senior EY workers and deputy headteachers were classified as 'middle leaders'; and the remaining EYPs were classified as 'practitioner leaders'. Early years advisers and childminders were retained as separate categories. Figure 2.3 indicates the average time spent by practitioners who worked for four or more days a week on different leadership and management activities, some of which they did simultaneously.

There are a number of striking patterns in the data if early years advisers and consultants are excluded from the analysis. The first is the inverse relationship between managing staff and time working with children, which also depends on seniority: practitioners in senior leadership positions spent less time with children and more time managing staff. The second is that despite this trend, overall 88 per cent of these practitioners still stated that they worked directly with children (this excludes EYPs working as advisers or consultants). Even senior leaders worked directly with children for at least one day a week on average. The third is the consistency with which leaders at every level were involved in leading, coordinating and evaluating practice in their settings.

The pattern of involvement in delivering and developing staff training and supporting their continuing professional development (CPD) was more complex. Just under half (48 per cent) of respondents routinely led training and professional development sessions in their settings. Experienced and senior leaders tended to be more involved but there was widespread engagement across leadership levels and career stages. Nearly three-quarters

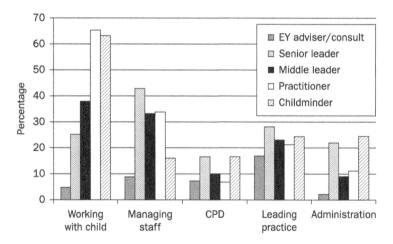

Figure 2.3 Percentage of time practitioners spent on different duties: national survey 2 (responses = 1,548).

(74 per cent) of respondents were given opportunities to share their own learning from the professional development activities they had undertaken in their settings. Opportunities to lead professional development outside their own settings were concentrated among senior leaders and more experienced professionals, with only one-fifth being involved routinely. Childminders were heavily involved, with just over half (52 per cent) leading professional development outside their settings, indicating their importance in supporting and developing local networks of practitioners.

The overall impression from the surveys was that, although these practitioners were distributed across a number of formal leadership categories, these categories were not quite as distinct as you would typically expect to find in the school sector. For example, leadership in the early years sector was far more 'hands-on' in terms of engagement in the everyday practices of the setting. These leaders worked frequently with children and practitioners, were centrally engaged in planning and implementing curriculum change, and were heavily involved in developing and delivering professional development. More fine-grained analysis, which differentiated between leaders working in private, voluntary, independent and maintained settings, found no statistically significant differences in the workload analyses according to type of setting. The key conclusion we drew from the survey was that the common strand of activities between the leaders in the case studies was sufficiently large to treat them as a single group, if we focused on their leadership of practice. It also suggested that the main differences we would encounter would be in the scope and scale of these leaders' practice leadership activities, rather than in their nature, making it possible to carry out a cross-case analysis of their involvement in changing and improving practice. As the aim of this analysis was not so much to produce generic characteristics of *what* effective leaders do, but to understand more *how* leaders set about raising the quality of provision, then a focus on a common strand would hopefully indicate how they responded differently to the contexts in which they found themselves, allowing us to explore their contextual sensitivity. Concentrating on their construction of practice leadership, the direct and indirect activities focused on improving the quality of practice in a setting, also allowed us to follow a common analytical thread across settings. This would help us to unravel the role played by their general approach to leadership and the differences that arose from their responses to contextual factors in shaping their leadership of practice.

The data from the survey suggested that leaders across the sector were trying to achieve similar standards and implement the same curriculum frameworks in very different contexts. The analysis suggested that a common 'strand' of leadership responsibilities and activities existed. This is perhaps not surprising considering recent policy priorities in the early years in England that have focused on a relatively small range of improvements. For example, the emphasis on supporting children's learning through child-initiated learning and play, including outdoor play, was a feature of the original Foundation Stage Guidance.[9] Improving early identification and intervention was another area that showed how a recurring policy focus, from Sure Start to funding for free pre-school places for two-year-olds, was shaping their view of quality provision.[10] In combination, such policies have resulted in additional scrutiny and greater prescription as to the nature and quality of the provision that should be on offer. A mixture of inspection pressures, new curricula and quality standards has created similar sets of external pressures on leaders across the sector. They have led to a degree of conformity in the aspects of practice they focused on in their leadership. We therefore hypothesised that this would place increased demands on leaders operating in diverse settings to deal with the internal and external factors they faced in bringing about similar improvements in practice.

Reanalysing the surveys led to two key developments in our approach. First, it showed that there was sufficient commonality among these leaders to suggest that the concept of practice leadership could provide a common analytical thread across settings. Second, this would allow us to explore differences in how these leaders affected the quality of provision and responded to the contextual factors that shaped their leadership.

Conceptualising how to lead practice

Once we had made the decision to treat the case study participants as one group of leaders, we developed our original questions further: How could we assess leaders' impact on quality in a way that would allow for comparisons across different settings and how would we study their different approaches to how they achieved these impacts without overlaying a pre-existing leadership approach? Our response to the first question was to create a single 'objective' assessment of quality that would be uniformly applied across the cases. The second question required us to adapt how logic models are used in leadership research. These approaches allowed us to combine the benefits of using an objective measure of impact with a means of developing our understanding of how leaders achieved such impacts in a way that would be contextually sensitive.

We will start with the issue of how to avoid overlaying an existing approach to leadership. The survey data had indicated that leaders across the sector were highly engaged in trying to influence the practice of others in their settings, both directly and indirectly. We wanted to capture their attempts at doing this – and the results of their efforts – in ways that would be sensitive to the contingent nature of leadership in the early years sector and also provide advice and support to policy makers and practitioners.

The following definition describes the leadership roles contained in the original EYPS standards. Practitioners were to act as:

> catalysts for change and innovation: they are key to raising the quality of early years provision and they exercise leadership in making a positive difference to children's wellbeing, learning and development.
>
> (CWDC, 2010: 17)

The standards were not intended to be a leadership development programme, but a means of improving the overall quality of provision. Therefore, they had spread their remit wide by stating they were targeted at those who were 'leading practice in their workplaces'.[11] This aspect of leadership was not developed in the standards, but it was stated that those leading practice would need to implement the EYFS,[12] which in effect set out a wide range of practices they needed to lead on and the level of quality they had to reach. As a result, what constituted quality provision was far more clearly articulated than how leaders should achieve it.

Therefore, while these practice leaders were described in the original standards as 'catalysts for change and innovation', there was no prescribed approach for how they should lead. This gap did not persist for long, as a range of writers and researchers, drawing on their own experiences, research and leadership constructs from other areas, set out to try to define the unique characteristics of this variation of early years leadership. Hallet and Roberts-Holmes (2010) described them as 'leaders of learning',[13] while Heikka and Waniganayake (2011) saw them in terms of pedagogical leadership, arguing that leading practice in early childhood leadership involves combining pedagogical and distributed forms of leadership, as these leaders are responsible for creating a community that fosters learning and communication. They also recognised that, in practice, pedagogical leadership is only one aspect of early years leadership and 'has to be considered within the full extent of leadership roles and responsibilities expected of today's early childhood leaders'.[14]

The problem with using existing leadership approaches and models such as pedagogical and distributed leadership to look at a single aspect of early years leadership, however, is that they tend to be overarching models that cover a range of overlapping activities and dispositions. This is because those involved in generating and defining such approaches tend to do so by looking for characteristics shared by effective leaders. In order to generate common characteristics and create coherent accounts of effective leadership, the final models lose the detail and subtlety found in more contextualised and procedural accounts. They also often fail to support practitioners in thinking about to how to improve practice 'in a setting like mine' because these models often become totalising, giving the impression that all elements of the models are equally important in all instances.

We wished to focus on a single aspect of early years leaders' activities, the leadership of practice, at different levels and across settings in ways that encapsulated the nuances and details of their leadership. At the same time, we needed to have sufficient read-across to produce generic guidance related to bringing about improvements across a range of settings. We wanted to use the notion of practice leadership as a tool for examining early years leadership in context. The intention was not to encapsulate all of the facets and dimensions of leadership, or to account for the various forms of 'capital' that leaders must accrue.[15] Instead, our focus was on one key aspect of a leader's role: the improvement of the quality of provision in a setting. This would allow us to consider in detail questions concerning the procedural, or 'how to', knowledge of leaders, and how they applied it in response to the opportunities and issues they faced in their settings.

Therefore, we decided to combine the 'objective' measures of quality we were developing not with a particular model of leadership but rather with a broad 'logic' model that would delineate key aspects of the links between leaders' activities, the development of practice leadership in their settings, improvements in quality, and outcomes for children. This broad logic model would also enable us explore the 'causality of improvement', i.e. the linkages between leadership practices and improved outcomes for children. Each case study of the development of practice leadership was in part a study of the 'local' nature of this causality and of the interactions associated with the direct and indirect impacts of leaders. Rather than relying simply on leaders' narratives of change, through the use of repeated objective measures of quality, it would explore how their actions brought about, directly and indirectly, changes in others.

The causal nature of leadership

The analytical use of causality in studies of leadership has long been problematic in that it has tended to result in generic accounts of effective leadership. Researchers interested in mapping the causality of leadership have popularised the use of logic models that set out 'causal chains' of factors that link leadership approaches to student outcomes.[16] These models rely on a specific notion of causality that allows those who use them to make statistical claims about the reliability and validity of their claims concerning the strengths of the links in the causal chains they describe. The notion of causality used in these traditional logic models is based on the twin ideas of repetition and 'regularity'.[17] Causality is assumed when there is a consistent and regular association between two factors. Hence, they rely on correlation between factors as a proxy for them being in a causal relationship. This reliance on regularity results in a somewhat dated and naive notion of how causality operates in complex social situations, which arises in part from an uncritical importation of a rather dated notion of causality from the natural sciences.[18] What is attractive about these 'logic' models is that the causal chains they draw between leaders' activities and impacts on quality are relatively broad. They are theoretically driven in the sense that what are seen as key links depends on the leadership theory that underpins them, but as these links often span multiple theories, what is more distinctive is the nature of the links between them. This means that the chains are to a degree theory-blind, in the sense that many of the key 'links' in these chains appear in various theories, allowing us to explore in our case studies how each leader set about chaining them together in their context.

Researching practice leadership required the development of a different kind of logic model, which would capture the 'local' nature of causation in each setting. The logic in these models would therefore be less that of statistical correlation and inference, more the causality of social processes that bring about change in practice. This would mean drawing on notions such as leaders' professional identities and values. The emphasis on social processes meant that it was unlikely that a single narrative of how improvements are created would emerge, but this does not necessarily undermine the 'truth' of claims that improvement had occurred. It is not a contradiction to combine 'objective' measures of quality with diverse accounts of the processes that brought about improvements. Indeed, it emerged that recognising and using the different narratives and understandings of those involved in settings is an important aspect of developing practice leadership.

A causal model approach to researching practice leadership

Our starting point for developing a causal model approach to studying practice leadership was to use a more contextualised and less deterministic notion of causality. The 'links' in the causal chains we were interested in making would be based on the interaction of different forms of individual and collective agency, taking into account notions of followers and resistors and the interplay of personal and organisational narratives. These links would be centrally concerned with the 'meaning' that these actions and interactions had for those in the chain. Differences in the meaning of each step in the chain would arise from a variety of sources, including the professional identity of individuals and the social nature of the processes of 'meaning making' required to bring about collective understanding and joint effort.

Various types of logic models, suggesting different sequences of unilateral and multilateral causal chains, have been developed to link leadership

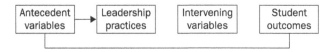

Figure 2.4 Mediated-effects model.

with improvements in children's outcomes.[19] Most of the research into school leadership, once it moves on from simplistic direct models of impact, relies on iterations of the basic mediated-effects model,[20] i.e. they recognise that leadership practices tend not to have a direct causal impact on pupil outcomes, but are mediated through other variables, as Figure 2.4 illustrates.

These 'intervening' variables may either support or hinder the impact of leadership: 'Some of those variables *moderate* (enhance or mute) leadership effects, others "link" or *mediate* leadership practices to pupils and their learning, the *dependent* variables in our proposed study'.[21] The model in Figure 2.5 illustrates how these different factor types can be incorporated into chains that link leadership practices and pupil outcomes.

Recently, more complex reciprocal models have been proposed, and used, to study the relationships and interactions between leadership and the initial context. Heck and Hallinger (2010) used such a model to look at how moves towards more collaborative leadership approaches affected both schools' capacity and outcomes for students (see Figure 2.6). The model proposed several relationships between initial leadership capacity and outcomes for pupils. This kind of modelling allowed them to demonstrate that there is a mutually reinforcing relationship between changes in leadership and capacity for improvement. They argued for an organic and reinforcing relationship between leadership and improvement capacity over time, occurring irrespective of initial leadership capacity or levels of achievement. Leadership and

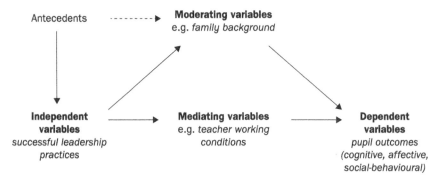

Figure 2.5 Example leadership logic chain.

Source: Day et al. (2006)

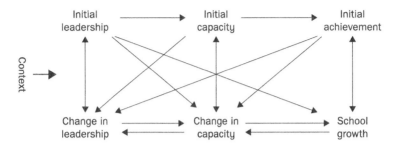

Figure 2.6   Reciprocal effects model of leadership and capacity building.

Source: Heck and Hallinger (2010)

improvement interacted with context but were not necessarily limited by initial conditions, which meant that all schools could theoretically improve by adopting certain leadership and capacity building approaches.

Reciprocal models such as this overcome the main limitations of earlier logic models, which were uni-directional and failed to capture the interaction between context, key variables and the nature of leadership. These reciprocal models, which tried to capture the interaction between context and approaches to leadership by setting them in a feedback loop, were first put forward over a quarter of a century ago by researchers such as Pitner (1988) (see Figure 2.7).

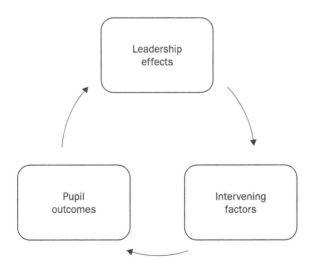

Figure 2.7   Reciprocal leadership model.

Source: Adapted from Pitner (1988)

Reciprocal models have not gained the same level of popularity as the more basic mediated effect models, largely because they are far less amenable to the forms of statistical analysis used to validate linear models and require more complex data collection frameworks operating over extended periods in order to capture the dynamics of the feedback loops and interactions between leadership and the changing context.

Although they support the argument for understanding more about how context and leadership interact, existing reciprocal logic model studies of leadership unfortunately tend to de-contextualise the leaders and schools they study. In order to generate the quality and quantity of data they require, they tend to rely on whole-school questionnaires, which use limited measures of leadership and capacity building, and amalgamate findings from a number of schools. This means that, although they can argue for the interaction of leadership and context, they cannot provide a great deal of detail about how this interaction operates, especially how it may be mutually reinforcing.

It was clear to us that some form of reciprocal model was needed to study practice leadership if we were to explore the 'local' nature of causation – how internal conditions in settings interacted with links in the chain between leaders' actions and improved outcomes for children. For example, staff morale might improve as children's behaviour improves, which might in turn lead to staff being more prepared to innovate. These changes to the intervening variables could affect leadership practices and allow more leadership energy to be directed to professional development and supporting staff to innovate. As this develops over time, leadership may become more distributed as staff develop more capacity to innovate. This in turn would generate qualitatively different staff interactions, including those with leaders.

The logic model used to study practice leadership in the early years sector had to be set in the wider contexts of locality and community, but it also had to indicate how changes to a setting's internal context affected its leadership. Our initial attempt to create a reciprocal model that linked aspects of individual and collective leadership with the leadership capacity of the setting and the process of improving quality is illustrated in Figure 2.8.

Retracing the causal chain

To investigate the specifics of how practice leaders operated in a given context, and make comparisons across 30 settings, required us to conceptualise each link in the chain in some detail. Any logic model can only suggest a number of possible pathways, or loops back, between leaders' actions and improved outcomes for children. The choice of which paths and links we explored needed to be informed by the existing research and knowledge base.

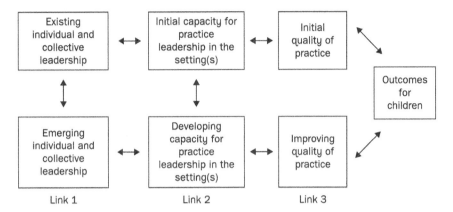

Figure 2.8 Reciprocal model of practice leadership.

In developing these links, we drew on both the existing early years knowledge base and also on research from other sectors.

Link 1: Existing and emerging leadership and developing capacity for practice leadership

The first link in the causal chain is the interaction between the existing leadership in the setting(s) and developing practice leaders. Studying practitioners who occupied different levels of the leadership hierarchies in settings required a model that could encompass the interaction between existing leadership, in all forms, and the emergence of practice leadership at different levels. The two-way direction of this link recognises that, as well as practice leaders being affected by the attitudes of existing leadership, they may in turn be affected by an increase in a setting's capacity for practice leadership. This might be a positive interaction, in that practice leadership may provide an entry point for new leaders and draw them into wider forms of leadership activities. However, it could also have a negative effect if the existing leadership fails to recognise these 'new' leaders. It is somewhat simplistic to discuss this interaction purely in terms of being a moderating or mediating influence, as the development of new leadership capacity might also affect existing leaders' approaches by encouraging them, for example, to adopt more distributed approaches to leadership. Chapters 5 and 6 contain exemplifications of such developments.

Link 2: Capacity for practice leadership and improvements to quality

This link is concerned with the relationship between increases in practice leadership and improvements to the quality of provision. We developed a model of quality improvement (see Figure 2.8) that recognised that practice leaders operated at various levels – senior, middle and practitioner – in the leadership hierarchies in their settings. The model recognised that different aspects of quality were more easily influenced depending on a leader's position in this hierarchy. So, senior leaders are more likely to be able directly to affect structural quality issues, such as staff-to-children ratios, wages and staff qualifications, than are more junior colleagues. In contrast, other aspects of quality, such as process quality issues, can be influenced directly by any practice leader by simply working alongside colleagues and modelling what was required of them. In terms of improving process quality, the model suggests that differences in leadership seniority affect the scope and scale of impacts, rather than their depth. The model was therefore an attempt to accommodate differences in practice leaders' influence on quality due to their position in the leadership structure of their setting, rather than due to the specific approach they took to leading practice.

Link 3: Quality and outcomes for children

The starting point for exploring the link between quality and outcomes was the concept of quality. The very different notions of quality used in the early years sector,[22] and the lack of robust empirical studies linking quality provision with longer-term outcomes for children, with the notable exception of studies such as EPPE and its extension into the Effective Pre-school Primary and Second Education (EPPSE) project, complicate the links between how leaders improve quality and how these improvements lead to gains in children's outcomes. Simplifying this complexity required the development of a model that linked improvements in quality to practice leadership and a fleshing-out of the empirical linkages between quality and outcomes for children.

The overall development of the model progressed backwards from impact to leadership activities and is discussed in this order in the following sections, starting with Link 3.

Link 3: Quality and outcomes for children – process, structures, proxies and surrogates

Our starting point for developing this link in more detail was to create an 'objective' measure of quality that was clearly associated with positive outcomes for children across settings. There are numerous models of quality, and an even wider range of quality frameworks and standards.[23] This has led to the argument that quality is more of a cultural construct than an objective measure.[24] As cultural constructs, definitions of quality arise from political and professional discourses and negotiations among stakeholders, so its meaning will vary depending on the different interests, views and power of these stakeholders (e.g. parents, children, providers, policy makers). In recognition that a variety of views exist on what constitutes quality, in each of the case studies we explored practice leaders' notions of quality and how central the idea of practice leadership was to their views of themselves as leaders. To make cross-case assessments of relative improvements in quality and link these to outcomes for pupils, we needed to develop a robust set of measures that could be applied to all the cases.

The model of quality developed as part of the research was 'objective' in the sense that it was based on combining the existing research evidence on the links between quality of provision and outcomes for children. The starting point for this model was to consider all the areas of a setting's provision on which practice leaders might potentially have a positive impact and to identify those areas of that impact that have been shown to have an impact on outcomes for children. The initial map of potential impacts on their settings is shown in Figure 2.9.

Our selection of the impacts to focus on drew on research into the links between quality and long-term outcomes for children. These links have been the subject of a number of sustained research programmes that have produced a considerable body of evidence showing how access to high quality early child education and care can make a significant difference to children's development and wellbeing.[25] Much of this research has been focused on the interrelation between quality and children's later learning experiences.[26] Longitudinal and concurrent studies have shown that high quality early childhood education can have a significant impact on children's learning, academic achievements, self-esteem and attitudes towards lifelong learning.[27] There is also substantial evidence that variations in the quality of education affect a wide range of cognitive, social and emotional outcomes in children's learning and development.[28] The next step was to consider what criteria and tools could be used to measure changes in the quality of each of these aspects of their settings consistently. The search for such criteria and tools meant that eventually we focused on a particular sub-set of all the potential areas of impact.

Drawing on this body of research, we used two sets of observational tools to assess quality across a range of the key areas of impact. The first was the Practitioner Child Interaction Tool (PCIT), based on schedules and process developed in the Researching Effective Pedagogy in the Early Years (REPEY) and Effective Early Learning (EEL) projects.[29] We used the PCIT to look for evidence that practitioners were engaging in pedagogical activities and practices that had been found to have an impact on outcomes for children in these earlier projects. The quality of the learning environment was assessed through the use of the Infant and Toddler Rating Scale (revised) (ITERS-R), the Early Childhood Environment Rating Scale Revised Edition (ECERS-R) and the Early Childhood Environment Rating Scale – Extension (ECERS-E), as used in the EPPE and REPEY projects and the Millennium Cohort Study.[30]

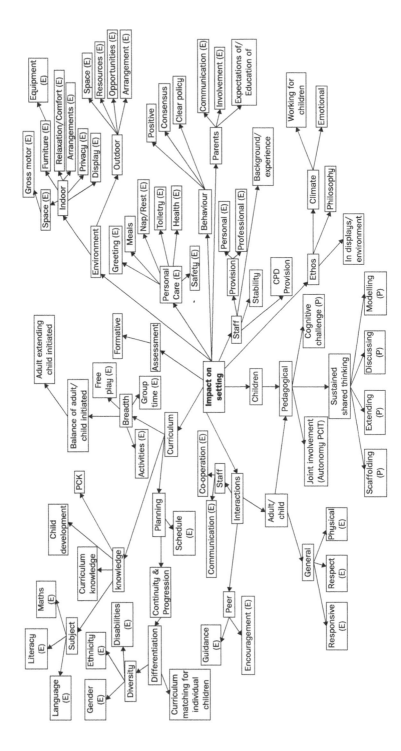

Figure 2.9 Initial map of potential areas of impact.

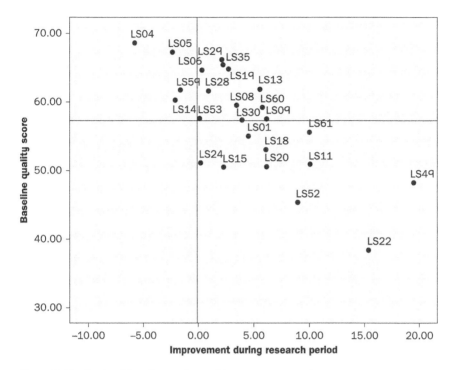

Figure 2.10   Settings' baseline quality and improvement over time.

We used these tools to provide objective measures of the quality of key areas of the settings' provision. We carried out a minimum of three sets of observations in each of the 30 settings over the three years, with multiple PCIT observations being carried out on each occasion. This allowed us to plot a trajectory between baseline and final quality scores and created an overall measure of improvement over the life of the study for the 25 settings for which we had sufficient reliable data.

The improvement axis on Figure 2.10 indicates the extent to which settings improved against their baseline measure of quality: the zero line indicates no overall improvement and a positive score indicates improvement from the baseline. The baseline quality score axis indicates the original assessment of the quality of the setting: the higher the score, the higher the initial quality of the setting. The crosshairs were created where the horizontal line that represents the mean baseline quality score crosses the vertical zero improvement line, which indicates no overall improvement in quality over the length of the study. Comparing these scores with the settings' final quality scores produced four improvement categories into which each setting was placed, which are mapped on the quadrant diagram in Figure 2.11. We used the

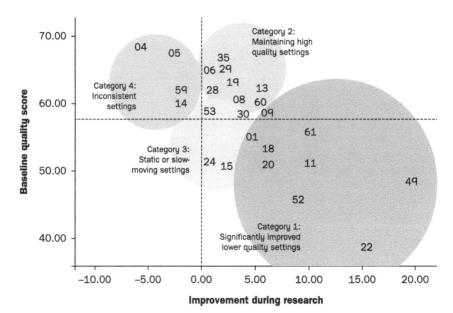

Figure 2.11 Case study settings' improvement groupings.

'LS' codes to identify the case study settings in the original research and we have retained them in this book to distinguish between settings. A full list of the case study settings and their key characteristics can be found in Appendix 1.

These four improvement categories were defined as follows:

Category 1   ***Significantly improved lower quality settings***
             Here the settings were originally below average but during the study they achieved significant improvements in terms of either framing pedagogies or pedagogical interactions (and sometimes both). (LS01, LS09, LS11, LS18, LS20, LS22, LS49, LS52, LS61)

Category 2   ***Maintaining high quality settings***
             This group contained settings that were initially above average in terms of baseline quality and maintained their position during the study. (LS06, LS08, LS13, LS19, LS28, LS29, LS35, LS60)

Category 3   ***Static or slow-moving settings***
             These were settings with below average or average levels of quality initially that appeared to be making slow progress, i.e. below the average final quality

score and with below average improvement. (LS15,
LS24, LS30, LS53)

Category 4   ***Inconsistent settings***
These settings initially exhibited above average
quality but had negative improvement scores at the
end of the study. (LS04, LS05, LS14, LS59)

The degree of improvement in quality scores varied considerably across
settings, with those initially baselined at the lower end of the quality scale,
generally rated by Ofsted as satisfactory, showing the greatest levels of
improvement. This was not surprising considering that those settings at the
higher end of the scale were all rated by Ofsted as outstanding and therefore
faced greater challenges in trying to improve their overall quality scores. The
four inconsistent settings, which showed a decline in quality over the period
of the study, were all baselined at the middle to high end of the quality
spectrum.

Link 2: Capacity for practice leadership and improvements to quality

Having developed a set of tools to provide an objective measure of quality in
each setting, and plotted their trajectories over time, we then needed to link
this to practice leadership. The model that was developed was based on a set
of assumptions about the agency of practice leaders, in terms of their ability
to affect different aspects of quality, and the definition of quality we used
drew on those that informed the creation of the observation tools. The model,
illustrated in Figure 2.12, had at its peripheries elements that required practice
leaders to hold more senior and strategic leadership roles in order to effect
substantive improvements.

In the model, practice leadership has the most direct link to process
quality, defined as 'the actual experiences that occur [. . .] including children's
interaction with caregivers and peers and their participation in different activities'.[31] It recognises that such activities are bounded by wider structural
quality factors, including staffing ratios, levels of staff qualifications, funding
for equipment and working conditions.[32] These are at the periphery of the
model because although some practitioners, for example owners and
managers, were in a sufficiently senior position to influence these factors,
many practice leaders in the case studies were not. The effectiveness of
practice leadership was therefore primarily measured by improvements in
process quality, rather than the structural quality in the setting.

The model differentiates between two aspects of process quality: pedagogical interactions and framing pedagogies. This interpretation of process

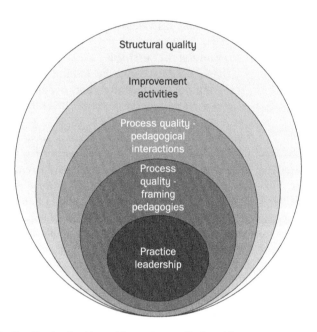

Figure 2.12   Practice leadership and improving quality in settings.

quality is adopted from the REPEY study, which defined pedagogical interactions as 'specific behaviours on the part of adults' and pedagogical framing as 'the behind-the-scenes aspects of pedagogy which include planning, resources, and establishment of routines'.[33] These categories were used to differentiate between improvements in background aspects of practice, such as planning, and practitioners' face-to-face interactions with children. Framing pedagogies were placed nearer the centre of the model to indicate that they were potentially more easily influenced by practice leaders of all levels. This assumption is based on prior research into professional development and school improvement that has emphasised that supporting practitioners to change their practice with children is more difficult than getting them to adopt changes that only affect their planning or preparation.[34] The model also recognised that the scope of the changes to process quality will depend on the scale and depth of practitioners' practice leadership, particularly their involvement in improvement activities such as staff training and curriculum development. The model allowed us to differentiate between practice leaders occupying different positions in settings' formal leadership hierarchy, if it was applied to each case with a sensitivity that recognised the interactions between the different types of quality. It had to be recognised that improvement to structural quality areas such as staff pay and qualifications might also affect process quality in areas such as interactions between staff and children.

The model helped clarify the links between practice and aspects of quality, especially those linked to longer-term outcomes for children. For example, pedagogical framing encompasses the behind-the-scenes aspects of pedagogy, including planning, resources and the environment, and the establishment of routines. Evidence from the EPPE study suggested that learning environments with a strong focus on both planning for individual learning needs and promoting understanding of cultural differences were effective in developing children's cognitive, social and behavioural development and helped to achieve better outcomes for all children.[35] The REPEY study demonstrated that the most effective early years settings achieved a balance between the opportunities provided for children to benefit from teacher-initiated group work and the provision of freely chosen yet potentially instructive play activities.[36] Beyond the provision of a 'balanced' curriculum, high quality pedagogical framing includes developing stimulating pedagogical environments and curricula that emphasise literacy, mathematics, science/environment and that cater for children of different genders, cultural backgrounds, abilities and interests.[37]

The REPEY study defined pedagogical interactions as:

> face to face interactions practitioners engage in with children; they may take the form of cognitive (mainly sustained shared thinking, direct teaching and monitoring) or social interactions (mainly encouragement, behaviour management, social talk and care).
>
> (Siraj-Blatchford et al., 2002: 7)

It also determined that a key aspect of high quality interactions, and the main difference between those settings it defined as 'good' and those defined as 'outstanding' was the extent to which practitioners engaged in sustained shared thinking (SST). This involves:

> episodes in which two or more individuals 'worked together' in an intellectual way to solve a problem, clarify a concept, evaluate activities or extend narratives. During a period of sustained shared thinking both parties contributed to the thinking and developed and extended the discourse.
>
> (Siraj-Blatchford and Sylva, 2004: 147)

The importance of SST to the quality of pedagogical interactions led to its inclusion as one of the core principles of learning and development in the EYFS.[38] All practitioners working with young children under five in England are therefore currently expected to promote and engage in SST. There is a strong correlation between the quality of interactions and the framing pedagogies in use. REPEY found that SST was much more likely to occur when children were interacting one-to-one with an adult or with another child and that freely chosen play activities often provided the best opportunities for adults to extend children's thinking.[39]

For many practice leaders, affecting the structural quality of settings would have been problematic unless they were owners or senior leaders. This is because improving on aspects of settings, such as staff-to-child ratios and staff qualifications and training, requires considerable influence over resources and policy. This is not to underplay the importance of structural issues; indeed, they could be a major influence on process quality. Our knowledge and understanding of how structural issues have an impact on quality in early childhood settings have been considerably enhanced by a number of recent studies, in particular the EPPE study and the Graduate Leader Fund (GLF) evaluation in the UK.[40] There is clear evidence that high quality early childhood education and care is linked to having a highly qualified, well-trained workforce. The highest quality provision has been found in settings that were led by a graduate, in particular by a teacher. For example, investigating outcomes for children in the Neighbourhood Nurseries Initiative found that the strongest predictor of positive behavioural and social outcomes for children was the involvement of a qualified teacher.[41] The EPPE study revealed a strong relationship between the qualifications of the setting manager and the quality of the setting, and the Millennium Cohort Study also found that the childcare qualifications of staff were a predictor of quality of provision, especially in aspects of provision which foster children's developing language, interactions and academic progress.

The number of trained staff in a setting and the type of training undertaken has also been found to be significant. Siraj-Blatchford and Manni (2007) found a positive correlation between higher proportions of formally qualified staff in a setting and higher quality provision, while Mathers et al. (2007) found that having a high proportion of unqualified staff had a negative effect on quality. The impact of more staff training and qualifications is also reported in research based in the USA and Northern Ireland.[42] There is therefore a clear relationship between structural and process quality. In studying practice leadership, structural quality was therefore treated as a key contextual factor. Throughout the cases, the staffing of each setting was monitored on each visit to assess overall levels of qualifications and rates of staff turnover. The main structural quality factor was staff turnover, which appeared to be key in those settings that failed to improve, possibly indicating an inability to build capacity over time.

The quality improvement model helped in unpicking the relative importance, and interactions, between the two aspects of process quality. To explore these interactions, another series of more fine-grained improvement categories was created by cross-referencing improvements in pedagogical framing (as measured by ITERS-R/ECERS-R) against improvements in pedagogical interactions (as measured by PCIT), as outlined in Figure 2.13.

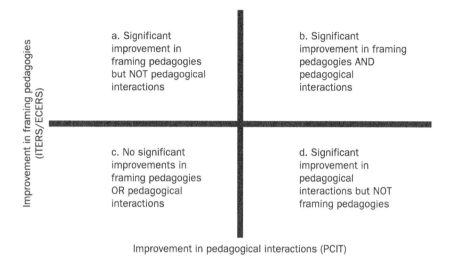

Figure 2.13 Improvement sub-categories.

Plotting all the category 1 settings into these categories produced Figure 2.14. Here, the crosswires were created by a horizontal line marking a significant improvement in pedagogical framing (an increase of 5 points or more from baseline to final ECERS-R or ITERS-R observation, which is equivalent to the 1 point increase regarded as significant in the GLF evaluation), and a vertical line, which marked a significant improvement in pedagogical interactions (where an improvement of 3 points in the aggregated PCIT data was regarded as significant). These improvements were deemed educationally significant in that they constituted substantive improvements in quality based on the categories used within each tool.

The bottom left quadrant is empty, indicating that all of the category 1 settings made significant improvements in relation to either framing pedagogies or interactions. The top right quadrant indicates that three settings (LS11, LS22 and LS49) made educationally significant improvements in both areas. The other six settings had made educationally significant improvements in either their framing or their interactions. The importance of this analysis is that the settings with the highest overall levels of improvement achieved this by improving *both* aspects of process quality. Possible reasons for these improvements are outlined in Chapters 4 and 5.

Similar analyses were carried out on the data from settings in the other categories and these indicated some interesting improvement patterns. In category 2 settings, which were already high quality at the beginning of the research, gains tended to be related to improvements in pedagogical interactions rather than framing pedagogies. Seven of these eight settings showed

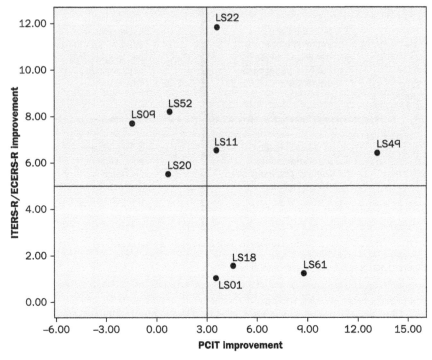

Figure 2.14 Category 1 settings' improvement on framing pedagogies (ITERS-R/ECERS-R) and pedagogical interactions (PCIT).

improvements on PCIT scores, three of which were significant, suggesting that they maintained and increased already high improvement levels through focusing on interactions with children. Those that showed improvements in their framing pedagogies tended to be in areas such as mathematics (in ECERS-E), which have been shown to have a positive impact on outcomes for children. This was further supported by the fact that the category 3 and 4 settings showed relatively small improvements in framing pedagogies in terms of ECERS-R and ITERS-R scores and, in the case of all but two settings which showed modest increases, declining scores in terms of interactions on the PCIT. Only one setting from these categories showed an educationally significant improvement (LS24 on ECERS-R) and this was matched by an almost corresponding decrease on the PCIT score.

The overall picture was that the majority of settings improved over the period of the study. Over time, the gap in quality between practice leaders and other practitioners' pedagogical interactions narrowed with the exception of the degree of cognitive challenge observed in the PCITs, which remained constant, demonstrating the difficulty of improving practice in this respect.

The trend in the ECERS-R and ITERS-R data was one of gradual improvement during the study. The sub-scales that contributed most to the improvement in ITERS-R were for interactions and listening and talking and, for ECERS-R, programme structure and interaction.

The settings that improved most were those where the focus was on improving both aspects of process quality: pedagogical interactions and pedagogical framing. The settings that improved in process quality also improved in those areas associated with positive long-term outcomes for children: literacy, mathematics and diversity all showed improvements, as did the frequency with which practitioners engaged in sustained shared thinking with children. In the following chapters, we discuss in detail how practice leaders brought about these improvements.

Link 1: Existing and emerging leadership and developing capacity for practice leadership

The relationship between the existing leadership of a setting, the practitioners in it who were awarded the status of practice leaders, and the broader development of a setting's capacity for practice leadership is complex. First, we were studying practitioners who occupied different levels of the leadership hierarchies in settings. This meant they were likely to have varying levels of influence on the existing leadership. Second, our sample contained a number of settings that had more than one practitioner with EYPS. Finally, existing leaders were likely to differ in their commitment to developing the quality of settings and to recognising and realising the potential of practice leaders. They also adopted a range of approaches to improving quality that may or not have supported the idea of developing broader leadership capacity. To help us conceptualise the interaction between existing leadership and the emergence of practice leadership at different levels, we drew on two existing research strands – research into teacher leadership[43] and research into capacity building in schools.[44]

We drew on teacher leadership research because it is concerned in particular with the socio-cultural interactions between existing levels of leadership and teachers' pedagogical leadership in the classroom. We saw these concerns as having strong parallels with the development of practice leadership at all levels. The key aspect of this research that was of interest was how existing leadership supported or hindered teachers taking a lead on developing their, and others', classroom practice. York-Barr and Duke's (2004) meta-synthesis of 25 years of teacher leadership research provided a useful summary of the key findings in those areas that had possible implications for the study of practice leadership. The key findings of their meta-synthesis are set out in Table 2.1 together with the implications for our study.

Table 2.1 Key findings about existing leadership and the development of teacher leadership

Key findings	Relevance to practice leadership
Certain models of leadership such as instructional, participative and distributed, are more inclusive of the concept of teacher leadership than others.	Do more inclusive approaches to leadership actually generate greater emphasis on improving practice?
Senior leaders play a pivotal role in the success of teacher leadership by actively supporting the development of teachers, by maintaining open channels of communication, and by aligning structures and resources to support the leadership work of teachers.	How do senior leaders set about creating the context and opportunities for practice leadership to develop at different levels in the settings?
Teacher leadership roles are often ambiguous and the likelihood of being successful is increased if roles and expectations are mutually shaped and negotiated with colleagues and other leaders on the basis of context-specific (and changing) instructional and improvement needs.	How do practice leaders' definition of the scope of their leadership differ at various levels in settings, and how central is the development of others' pedagogical practices to this definition?
Existing professional norms at different levels can either challenge or support the emergence of teacher leadership.	Do existing professional norms at different levels in settings challenge or support the emergence of practice leadership?
Developing trusting and collaborative relationships, both vertically and horizontally, is the primary means by which teacher leaders influence their colleagues.	How important is the development of collaborative professional networks in settings to the creation of leadership relationships at different levels?
Teacher leadership work that is focused at the classroom level of practice is likely to show student effects more readily than work focused at the organizational level.	How important is it that practice leadership develops at all levels within a setting, in terms of bringing about widespread improvement in the quality of provision?

Source: Adapted from York-Barr and Duke (2004)

The research on teacher leadership highlights many of the issues between existing leaders and the development of practice leadership as an organisational capacity. Studying how these issues might play out in practice and affect the development of this capacity also involved drawing on the literature on capacity building.

The concepts of organisational capacity and capacity building are relatively new in education. Various models have been developed to try and encapsulate their key features.[45] One of the foundational models was created by

Mitchell and Sackney (2000) and was based on three nested levels of capacity: individual, interpersonal (or team) and organisational.[46] Building capacity at each level requires different types of development, from individuals acquiring new knowledge and skills, through the creation of a shared understanding of appropriate norms in teams, to the promotion of an organisational ethos and culture that support development and risk taking.

Mitchell and Sackney (2000) treated capacity building as a process of developing human and social capital simultaneously. They warned that it did not matter at which level one started to build capacity, but that it was vital to work at all three. What is striking looking back now at their model is how interpersonal capacity is limited to the formal team structure of organisations. More recent research into leadership and organisational development (for example, Spillane and Kim, 2012) has stressed the importance of leaders' positioning within the informal networks in organisations.[47] Informal professional networks are seen as key in creating new, and directing existing, capacity towards shared improvement foci. The other striking element of the model is that it limits the boundaries of capacity building to the organisation itself. Again, more recent research has highlighted the importance of the personal and professional network of individual leaders and practitioners in providing them with support and information.[48] Moreover, a range of partnerships, chains and links between organisations across education sectors and systems has shown how effectively focused collaborative activities can build capacity at all levels.[49]

We treated the study of the development of leadership capacity as an investigation into a form of networked social capital. The social capital being exchanged was knowledge of new practices and support to undertake improvements. We drew on social network analysis (SNA) to map the growth of the relationships between leaders and practitioners in the settings that were marked by different types of exchanges.[50] This was undertaken via a series of short questionnaire surveys that were distributed to all staff in the settings. The questionnaires asked staff about whom they interacted with in the setting when they sought different forms of advice and support. The questions were structured so that they progressively explored interactions that increased in the depth of knowledge and support on offer and their intensity over time. They progressed from asking about which staff they had approached for general advice or specific support around leading change and improving practice to those interactions they felt had substantively changed their practice. Practice leaders were also asked additional questions about their wider professional networks outside of their settings.

The responses were used to create a series of sociograms that illustrated the shifting connections between practitioners in each setting and the density of their professional relationships. The analysis of these sociograms revealed the connectedness and centrality of the practice leaders in the professional networks in each case study setting, and also tracked the emergence of new leaders. Let us look at one practice leader and the sociograms her settings produced in order to demonstrate how they helped track the development of practice leadership capacity. In this particular setting, the practice leader was Rebecca. When practitioners were asked in the first SNA survey who they were most likely to talk to about their work with children or routine work-related issues, a fairly high degree of reciprocity was apparent among the nursery workers and this included Rebecca. This was despite the fact that this was one of five settings for which she was responsible and her office was in a separate building from the nursery in which the other staff worked. Despite this, in the interview data she expressed her frustration at not being able to spend as much time in the setting as she would have liked and she felt the other practitioners needed. This became a priority for her and when the SNA survey was repeated a year later and practitioners were asked about more formal support, such as who had mentored them at work in the previous 12 months, Rebecca was the most central figure in the setting's network, followed by its supervisor, reflecting her success in prioritising her work to support others' practice (see Figure 2.15).

By repeating these social network analyses over time, it was possible to chart the development of many of the professional networks in the settings. This allowed us also to map the developing role of the practice leader, as well as the sub-networks they supported and which supported each other. These data therefore provided additional evidence of a growing capacity for practice leadership in a setting by revealing whether or not there was a growing number of staff to whom individuals went for support to help them improve their practice. The sociograms provided an important form of triangulation

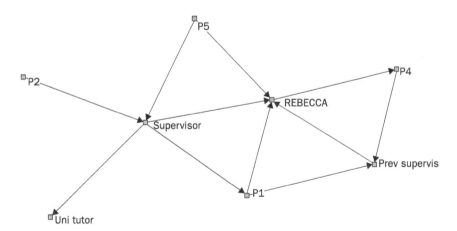

Figure 2.15 People who have mentored you in the last 12 months (LS08 SNA survey 2).

that could be set against practice leaders' narratives about what they were attempting to do in their settings and the actual impact of their formal and informal capacity building and improvement practices.

Summary

By the end of our initial period of research, our understanding of practice leaders and how they had constructed practice leadership had moved some distance. We had started with a group of practitioners who had been declared to be 'practice leaders' by dint of acquiring EYPS. Looking at this self-selected sample it became clear that they shared a common core, or strand, of leadership activities. Although this strand differed in scope and scale depending on their position within the formal leadership hierarchies of their settings, its focus on working with staff and children to improve the quality of practice became a lens through which we could look in more detail at how they adapted their leadership to their contexts. Identifying a single aspect of their leadership also helped focus the case studies we were developing of 'how' practice leaders brought about improvements in settings. We were also keen to ensure that we did not rely solely on leaders' narratives about the impact they had on the quality of the practice in their setting. Therefore, we linked the evidence we collected from them with more objective measures of quality. To do this we created a simple improvement model that linked practice leaders' actions to different aspects of quality, which we were able to measure consistently across settings. To unpick leaders' accounts and draw in additional data, such as from the social network analysis, we used a reciprocal logic model that linked existing leaders to the development of practice leadership and then to improvements in quality and outcomes for children.

In the following chapters, we use a range of data from cases studies and surveys to explore this notion of practice leadership in more detail. In Chapter 3, we discuss the development of both practice leaders and leadership capacity before moving onto more detailed accounts of how these leaders succeeded, or failed, to make an impact on the quality of practice in their settings.

Notes

1   Teaching Agency (2012a) *Review of the Early Years Professional Status Standards*. London: Teaching Agency.
2   Children's Workforce Development Council (CWDC) (2010) *On the Right Track: Guidance to the Standards for the Award of Early Years Professional Status*. Leeds: CWDC, at p. 17.

3   See, for example, Southworth, G. (2004) *Primary School Leadership in Context: Leading Small, Medium and Large Sized Primary Schools*. London: Routledge Falmer.

4   Southworth (2004); Southworth, G. (1998) *Leading Improving Primary Schools: The Work of Headteachers and Deputy Heads*. London: Falmer Press; Spillane, J., Halverson, R. and Diamond, J. (2004) Towards a theory of leadership practice: a distributed perspective, *Journal of Curriculum Studies*, 36 (1), 3–34.

5   Mathers, S., Ranns, H., Karemaker, A.M., Moody, A., Sylva, K., Graham, J. and Siraj-Blatchford, I. (2011) *Evaluation of Graduate Leader Fund: Final Report*. London: DfE.

6   Hadfield, M., Jopling, M., Royle, K. and Waller, T. (2011) *First National Survey of Practitioners with Early Years Professional Status*. London: CWDC; Hadfield, M. and Jopling, M. (2012) *Second National Survey of Practitioners with Early Years Professional Status Report*. Research Report DFE-RR239a. London: DfE.

7   Teaching Agency (2012b) *Early Years Professional Status Standards (from September 2012)*. London: Teaching Agency.

8   Aubrey, C. (2011) *Leading and Managing in the Early Years*, 2nd edn. London: Sage; Rodd, J. (2006) *Leadership in Early Childhood: The Pathway to Professionalism*. Buckingham: Open University Press.

9   Department for Education and Employment (DfEE) (2000) *Curriculum Guidance for the Foundation Stage*, London: Qualifications and Curriculum Authority.

10 For Sure Start, see Siraj-Blatchford, I., Clarke. K. and Needham, M. (eds.) (2007) *The Team Around the Child*. Stoke-on-Trent: Trentham Books; and for funding for pre-school places for two-year-olds, see Department for Education (DfE) (2014a) *Early Years Pupil Premium and Funding for two-year-olds*. London: DfE.

11 CWDC (2010), at p. 3.

12 See Department for Education (DfE) (2011) *Statutory Framework for the Early Years Foundation Stage*. London: DfE; Department for Education (DfE) (2014b) *Statutory Framework for the Early Years Foundation Stage: Setting the Standards for Learning, Development and Care for Children from Birth to Five*. London: DfE.

13 Hallet, E. and Roberts-Holmes, G. (2010) *The contribution of the Early Years Professional Status role to quality improvement strategies in Gloucestershire: Final Report*. Unpublished Manuscript, Institute of Education, University of London.

14 Heikka, J. and Waniganayake, M. (2011) Pedagogical leadership from a distributed perspective within the context of early childhood education, *International Journal of Leadership in Education: Theory and Practice*, 14 (4), 499–512, at p. 499.

15 Hargreaves, D.H. (2001) A capital theory of school effectiveness and improvement, *British Educational Research Journal*, 27 (4), 487–503.

16 See, for example, Hallinger, P. and Heck, R.H. (2011) Conceptual and methodological issues in studying school leadership effects as a reciprocal process, *School Effectiveness and School Improvement*, 22 (2), 149–73.

17 Maxwell, J. (2012) The importance of qualitative research for causal explanation in education, *Qualitative Inquiry*, 18 (8), 655–61.

18 Ibid.

19 See Heck, R.H. and Hallinger, P. (2010) Collaborative leadership effects on school improvement, *The Elementary School Journal*, 11 (2), 226–52.

20 Muijs, D. (2011) Researching leadership: towards a new paradigm, in T. Townsend and J. MacBeath (eds.) *International Handbook of Leadership for Learning*, New York, NY: Springer.

21 See Day, C., Kington, A., Stobart, G. and Sammons, P. (2006) The personal and professional selves of teachers: stable and unstable identities, *British Educational Research Journal*, 32 (4), 601–16.

22 See, for example, Cottle, M. and Alexander, E. (2012) Quality in early years settings: government, research and practitioners' perspectives, *British Educational Research Journal*, 38 (4), 635–54; Mathers et al. (2011).

23 Mathers et al. (2011).

24 Tobin, J. (2005) Quality in early childhood education: an anthropologist's perspective, *Early Education and Development*, 16 (4), 422–34.

25 Mooney, A., Boddy, J., Statham, J. and Warwick, I. (2008) Approaches to developing health in early years settings, *Health Education*, 108 (2), 163–77.

26 Sheridan, S. (2007) Dimensions of pedagogical quality in preschool, *International Journal of Early Years Education*, 15 (2), 197–217.

27 Sylva, K. (1994) School influences on children's development, *Child Psychology and Psychiatry*, 35 (1), 135–70; NICHD Early Child Care Research Network (2002) Early child care and children's development prior to school entry: results from the NICHD Study of Early Child Care, *American Educational Research Journal*, 39, 133–64; Burchinal, M.R., Peisner-Feinberg, E., Bryant, D.M. and Clifford, R. (2000) Children's social and cognitive development and child care quality: testing for differential associations related to poverty, gender, or ethnicity, *Journal of Applied Developmental Sciences*, 4, 149–65.

28 Siraj-Blatchford, I., Sylva, K., Muttock, S., Gilden, R. and Bell, D. (2002) *Researching Effective Pedagogy in the Early Years*. Research Report DFES-RR356. London: DfES; Sylva, K., Melhuish, E., Sammons, P., Siraj-Blatchford, I. and Taggart, B. (2004) *The Final Report: Effective Pre-School Education*. Technical Paper 12: The Effective Provision of Pre-School Education (EPPE Project). London: Institute of Education, University of London/DfES; Mathers, S. and Sylva, K. (2007) *National Evaluation of the Neighbourhood Nurseries Initiative: The Relationship between Quality and Children's Behavioural Development*. Research Report SSU/2007/FR/022. London: DfES.

29 Pascal, C. and Bertram, T. (1997) *Effective Early Learning: Case Studies in Improvement*. London: Hodder & Stoughton.

30 For the revised ITERS-R, see Harms, T., Cryer, D. and Clifford, R.M. (2003) *Infant/Toddler Environment Rating Scale – Revised*. New York, NY: Teachers College Press; for the revised edition (ECERS-R), see Harms, T., Clifford, R. and Cryer, D. (1998) *Early Childhood Environment Rating Scale* (revised edn.). New York, NY: Teachers College Press; and for the ECERS – Extension, see Sylva, K., Siraj-Blatchford, I. and Taggart, B. (2003) *Assessing Quality in the Early Years: Early Childhood Environment Rating Scale-Extension (ECERS-E): Four Curricular Subscales*. Stoke-on Trent: Trentham Books; and Mathers, S., Sylva, K., Joshi, H., Hansen, K., Plewis, I., Johnson, J., George, A., Linskey, F. and Grabbe, Y. (2007) *Quality of Childcare Settings in the Millennium Cohort Study*. London: HMSO.

31 Vandell, D.L. and Wolfe, B. (2000) Childcare quality: does it matter and does it need to be improved?, *Institute for Research on Poverty Special Report*, 78, 1–110, at p. 3.

32 Mooney, A., Cameron, C., Candappa, M., McQuail, S., Moss, P. and Petrie, P. (2003) *Early Years and Childcare International Evidence Project: Quality*. London: DfES.

33 Sylva, K., Melhuish, E., Sammons, P., Siraj-Blatchford, I. and Taggart, B. (2010) *Early Childhood Matters: Evidence from the Effective Pre-school and Primary Education* Project. London: Routledge, at p. 43.

34 See, for example, Reynolds, D. (1999) School effectiveness, school improvement and contemporary educational policies, in J. Demaine (ed.) *Contemporary Educational Policy and Politics*. London: Macmillan; Hopkins, D. (2001) *School Improvement for Real*. London: RoutledgeFalmer.

35 Sylva et al. (2004).

36 Siraj-Blatchford et al. (2002).

37 Sylva et al. (2004).

38 Department for Children, Schools and Families (DCSF) (2008) *Building Brighter Futures: Next Steps for the Children's Workforce*. London: DCSF.

39 Siraj-Blatchford, I., Sylva, K., Muttock, S., Gilden, R. and Bell, D. (2002) *Researching Effective Pedagogy in the Early Years*. Research Report DFES-RR356. London: DfES.

40 For the EPPE study, see Sylva et al. (2010); and for the GLF evaluation, see Mathers et al. (2011).

41 Mathers and Sylva (2007).

42 Peisner-Feinberg, E.S. and Burchinal, M.R. (1997) Relations between preschool children's child-care experiences and concurrent development: the Cost, Quality, and Outcomes Study, *Journal of Developmental Psychology*, 43, 451–77; Melhuish, E., Quinn, L., Hanna, K., Sylva, K., Siraj-Blatchford, I., Sammons, P. and Taggart, B. (2006) *The Effective Pre-school Provision in Northern Ireland Project, Summary Report*. Belfast: Stranmillis University Press.

43   York-Barr, J. and Duke, K. (2004) What do we know about teacher leadership? Findings from two decades of scholarship, *Review of Educational Research*, 74 (3), 255–316; Harris, A. and Muijs, D. (2005) *Improving Schools through Teacher Leadership*. Maidenhead: Open University Press.

44   Hadfield, M., Chapman, C., Curryer, I. and Barrett, P. (2001) *Capacity Building for Leadership and School Improvement*. Nottingham: National College for School Leadership.

45   See for example, Hadfield et al. (2001).

46   Mitchell, C. and Sackney, L. (2000) *Profound Improvement: Building Capacity for a Learning Community*. Lisse, Netherlands: Swets & Zeitlinger.

47   Spillane et al. (2004).

48   Daly, A., Moolenaar, N., Bolivar, J. and Burke, P. (2010) Relationships in reform: the role of teachers' social networks, *Journal of Educational Administration*, 48 (1), 359–91.

49   See Fullan, M. (2004) *Systems Thinkers in Action: Moving Beyond the Standards Plateau*. Nottingham: DfES.

50   The mapping used Borgatti, S.P., Everett, M.G. and Freeman, L.C. (2002) *Ucinet for Windows: Software for social network analysis*. Harvard, MA: Analytic Technologies [http://www.gse.harvard.edu/news/uk/09/05/treating-instructional-core-education-rounds].

3 Developing practice leaders and leadership capacity

This chapter focuses on the development of individual practice leaders and the associated idea of a setting's capacity for practice leadership. Exploring these ideas requires us to unpick the relationship between the existing leadership of a setting and the development of practice leaders, which is the first link in the causal model described in the previous chapter. The relationship between the existing leadership, the development of individuals as practice leaders, and the capacity of a setting is complex because it combines elements of both support and challenge. The research case studies contained instances where building leadership capacity was at the core of the formal leaders' approach to improving quality, as well as examples of practice leaders whose views of what constituted quality provision challenged formal leaders' norms and routines and led to resistance from them. Similarly, while some practice leaders were supported in their aspirations to develop others, including helping them take responsibility for elements of practice leadership, others were constrained by a lack of recognition from the formal leadership of their setting and were unable to bring about the broader impacts they sought.

We have used the idea of a setting having a certain capacity for practice leadership to make a distinction between the development of individual practice leaders and the ability of teams in a setting, or the setting as whole, to make improvements to practice. A setting's capacity for practice leadership is defined as its collective ability to bring about improvements in practice that have a positive impact on the quality of provision. Whether a setting builds this capacity depends on a number of factors ranging from the individual to the organisational. They include individuals' developing sense of themselves as practice leaders; the extent to which practice leaders are recognised and supported as leaders by others; and the professional networks in and between settings that support practitioners in improving their everyday practices.

A developing sense of being a practice leader

Our starting point for thinking about the development of individuals as practice leaders was to recognise the important role played by their professional identities. In many instances, they had developed these identities during their earlier careers as practitioners, although most were affected by the requirement to become practice leaders.

The survey responses indicated that practitioners who gained EYPS were drawn from all career stages.[1] Although the overall distribution was biased towards those in the early stages of their careers, the greatest proportion, 34 per cent, was made up of practitioners with 8–15 years' experience who therefore had established professional identities. Despite this, approximately three-quarters of them felt that gaining EYPS had changed their sense of professional identity since it had increased their status among other professionals, enhanced their confidence in developing colleagues and improved their ability to make improvements in their settings. Although many were established leaders, these and the other positive outcomes they reported after gaining EYPS meant that, for many, gaining the status represented a time of considerable change and/or consolidation in their professional identities.[2]

The survey highlighted the extent to which professional identities are part of an ongoing process of social negotiation and change in response to individual and contextual factors.[3] Recent research into professional identity in the early years has argued for a multiplicity of contextual influences as well as broader influences such as professional discourses and political ideologies.[4] Miller has also proposed that an individual's sense of professional identity is influenced by engagement in certain practices, arguing for a complex set of interactions between agency and identity. In our research, we adopted a similar position, arguing that individuals' identities would be linked to their agency as practice leaders, as identity is 'derived from status and position in the nursery, developing qualifications and knowledge base and the respect and confidence they commanded from others'.[5] We treated leaders' professional identities as existing in a reciprocal relationship with their professional agency, defined as their ability to enact their sense of themselves as leaders in settings and the professional networks in which they operated. Identity is thus formed through the interplay between what practice leaders think they should be doing and what they are actually able to do in practice in a given context. Our approach to researching practice leaders' developing sense of themselves as leaders was guided by the need to study this interplay.

The research revealed that the development of individual practice leaders was closely related to various shifts in the dynamic relationship between identity and agency. These shifts had a number of origins but, for many in our research, the completion of EYPS had initiated a new dynamic. In the survey, over 90 per cent reported that it had enhanced their knowledge and skills and given them a more critical understanding of practice, which in turn had improved their ability to share their existing knowledge with other colleagues: '*I felt I could impart the knowledge that I had because I could back it up through theory and research*' (Senior early years worker, voluntary setting). This practice leader felt more confident about imparting her views about what constituted good practice and what was the 'right' thing to do in the setting because she could now justify them on more substantive grounds than merely her own professional experiences. The connection between a more secure knowledge base and a growing sense of being a practice leader resonated throughout the survey responses. In the case studies, even very experienced practitioners, who had held a senior management position for some time, claimed that gaining EYPS had improved their ability to develop the quality of practice in their settings:

> *I now feel able to challenge colleagues and improve their perform-ance in a constructive and effective way, I feel I have a solid base on which to establish good leadership plus the skills to develop indi-viduals, embedding change at a caring and sensible pace that improves the performance of others whilst improving outcomes for children.*
>
> (Owner/manager, private setting)

The above quotation reveals a key social practice that shaped the dynamic between agency and identity. The ability to stimulate new learning within existing professional relationships was a key part of practice leaders' devel-opment because it balanced their need as leaders to challenge the existing practices in the setting without destabilising the established working relation-ships from which, in part, they drew their professional identity and status:

> *It has meant that, while working to improve practice in the setting, I am able to use my colleagues' existing skills and develop them in a way that empowers them and maintains a good working relationship.*
>
> (Senior early years worker, voluntary setting)

The relationship between professional identity and agency

Treating professional identity and agency as emerging out of a socially dynamic and contested process means studying them over time. In addition, as an individual's view of what constitutes 'good practice' and professionally appropriate leadership actions is influenced by the culture and existing prac-tices of the contexts in which they operate, and the relationships they have with colleagues, studies of leadership also need to be sensitive to context.[6] The relationship between professional identity and agency is therefore mediated, and moderated, by the professional norms and interactions that constitute a leader's setting. Over time, the history of change in a setting will influence the willingness of others to engage with a leader's change agenda and to learn from them. This will mean that a setting's history of improvement successes, or failures, will not only affect leaders' sense of self-efficacy, but also their social construction as leaders in that setting. This history will also affect the setting's collective capacity for practice leadership, meaning that collective agency will also be in dynamic relationship with the shared identity of those in the setting.

There are also wider influences on leaders' professional identities, beyond what has occurred in a setting or their professional histories. For example, McGillivray has emphasised the significance of community narratives, as these 'narratives are the starting point for some entering the workforce and will be continued by the working communities'.[7] Such community narratives are important not only in forming and maintaining identities (McGillivray, 2011), but also in shaping common understandings and establishing the professional language required to articulate and communicate to others the nature of professionalism in the early years sector.[8] Professional identity is therefore not only formed and located in specific settings but also through wider professional narratives and social discourses. For example, when practitioners were asked to what extent they felt gaining EYPS had affected their professional status, an overwhelming majority, 85 per cent, felt it had improved their status, especially with colleagues (72 per cent).[9] However, they also felt that there had been little recognition of their new status beyond their setting(s). Sixty-eight per cent of practitioners felt that other professionals they encountered did not recognise the status and 91 per cent felt that this was the case with people outside the early years sector.

Individuals' professional identities as practice leaders, and their sense of agency, are therefore shaped by their actions and interactions with others and through the narratives they create about their day-to-day work and the narratives in which they are positioned by others. Figure 3.1 attempts to illustrate the dynamic between practice leaders' identity and agency, underlining the fact that it is influenced not only by their settings but also by the broader professional networks from which they receive direct and indirect support.

The model highlights the extent to which individuals' approach to practice leadership in their settings is shaped by the dynamic between their developing sense of being a leader and their ability to enact change. It recognises that professional identity is formed and located not just in practitioners' specific contexts and situations, but also in their biographies and broader experiences. Identity is important in that it has an indirect and reciprocal relationship with their construction of their leadership roles. Furthermore, the

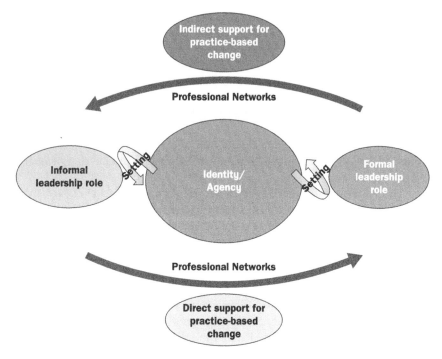

Figure 3.1 Identity formation, individual and collective agency.

ways in which practitioners view practice leadership, from what constitutes improved practice to how this is best achieved, shapes the scope and range of activities they undertake.

What were the key contextual factors?

In our original research, we explored the contextual influences that shaped the development of practice leaders by asking them what supported or hindered their ability to bring about improvements in their settings. The survey data not only provided a comprehensive overview of the importance practitioners placed on a number of factors, but also allowed us to make comparisons among practitioners at various career stages and working in different types of setting. Four general types of factors emerged from the surveys, as Table 3.1 illustrates.

The overall analysis (see Figure 3.2) revealed that the key contextual issues were cultural, specifically staff attitudes. Staff members' reluctance to change their practice was the only challenge that the majority of practitioners (53 per cent) agreed was an issue in their setting. Of the structural challenges,

Table 3.1 Barriers to improvement

Category	Barrier
Cultural	Colleagues' reluctant to change practice Colleagues unreceptive to new ideas
Structural	Lack of resources in the setting Lack of staff to try anything new
Leadership	Leaders did not recognise need to change Leaders lacked sufficient authority to bring about change Leaders within the setting did not listen to their advice about the need to improve
Community	The nature of the local community made it difficult to make improvement Difficulties in engaging parents

lack of resources (34 per cent) was mentioned more frequently than staffing levels (18 per cent). In terms of leadership, all three aspects represented a challenge to a clear minority of practitioners, with lack of authority being the most frequently mentioned (24 per cent).

Practitioners' positions in the overall structures of their settings affected the extent to which they regarded leadership issues as major barriers. Senior and middle leaders were less likely to report problems with colleagues who

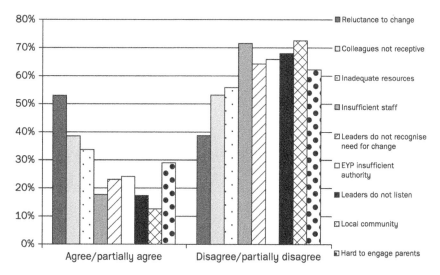

Figure 3.2 Barriers to improvement (responses = 1,769–1,781).

were reluctant to change or less receptive to new ideas than practice leaders with less formal leadership responsibility, although these differences were not always statistically significant. Similarly, those with less experience, especially novices (0–3 years) and those establishing themselves (4–7 years), were slightly more likely to report these as issues than those who were more experienced. Perhaps unsurprisingly, those who were lower in the leadership hierarchies were more likely to highlight problems with leaders who did not listen to their advice or recognise that changes were necessary. They also identified their lack of authority to effect change as an issue more frequently.

The type of setting in which leaders worked affected the structural and community barriers identified. Practitioners in voluntary settings were most likely to record lack of resources as a barrier to improvement (41 per cent regarded this as a barrier). Engaging parents was the most commonly cited community factor, identified by 29 per cent of practitioners, but this was highlighted far less frequently by childminders and those based in independent settings.

Asked to identify the single biggest challenge that they faced, a more complex picture emerged. Although staff reluctance to change was still the single most widely mentioned issue, challenges from all the categories dominated their concerns, as Table 3.2 indicates.

Again, practitioners' responses varied considerably depending on the type of setting in which they worked and their leadership positions. For example, the cultural issue of individuals' reluctance to change was the most difficult challenge for 31 per cent of practitioners in private settings, but only 20 per cent of staff in local authority settings. There were more distinct patterns when structural and leadership challenges were considered.

Table 3.2 Most difficult barriers to overcome

Statement	Frequency	Percentage	Barrier type
Individuals reluctant to change	379	25	Cultural
It is hard to engage parents in my setting(s)	278	19	Community
My setting(s) does not have adequate resources to implement changes	226	15	Structural
Colleagues not receptive to new ideas	167	11	Cultural
Insufficient authority to bring about improvements	166	11	Leadership
Leaders do not recognise changes necessary	100	7	Leadership
Nature of my local community makes it difficult to make improvements	67	5	Community
Not enough staff to try anything new	55	4	Structural
Leaders do not listen to my advice	62	4	Leadership

In voluntary and community settings, lack of resources was the major challenge faced by 20 per cent of leaders, while it was mentioned by only 10 per cent in the maintained sector and 11 per cent of those in local authority settings. The situation was reversed in relation to leadership issues. Lacking the authority to bring about change was the most difficult challenge to overcome for 22 per cent of respondents in maintained and local authority settings, while it was seen as such by only 8 per cent in private settings and 6 per cent in voluntary and community settings. Again, some responses demonstrated clear variations in perspective between those holding different positions in leadership structures. Over a quarter of senior leaders (27 per cent) rated parental engagement as the most significant barrier they faced. Practitioners without major leadership responsibilities rated it far lower than on average, at only 9 per cent.

In terms of moderating factors, those that hindered practice leadership, two key contextual factors emerged: the nature of the setting, which in particular affected the structural issues leaders faced; and their position in the formal leadership structure of settings, which affected the extent to which they could address cultural issues and develop authority. Together these two factors determined the extent to which they were recognised as leaders, had the confidence of others and could use organisational structures and processes to embed their notions of professionalism and effective practice in the setting.

In summary, these practice leaders faced a complex mix of organisational barriers that limited their ability to bring about improvements in their settings. They included cultural, structural, community and leadership issues. The relative significance of these to individual practice leaders depended as much, if not more, on the type of setting that they worked in as on their position in its formal leadership structure. The noticeable exceptions were those occupying the lower levels of leadership structures. They were more likely to see their perceived lack of authority to effect change as the biggest limitation on their agency. The notion that it was necessary for practice leaders to establish a position in the leadership structures – both formal and informal – of a setting underpinned our analysis of their development.

The developmental arc: becoming, being, developing

The survey data gave us some idea of the major contextual factors that shaped the dynamic between practice leaders' identity and agency and the contexts in which they worked, but could not tell us how this dynamic influenced their developmental 'arc' as leaders. However, it did indicate how long they had occupied their current leadership positions. The survey indicated that 49 per cent had only been in their current role for three years or less, with just 16 per cent having been in role for more than ten years. Thus, nearly half of these practice leaders could be regarded as still establishing themselves in their formal leadership positions. Those who were most likely to be in this position were those occupying the lower rungs of the formal leadership structures, the practitioner leaders, of whom 70 per cent had been in post for less than three years, as Figure 3.3 illustrates.

In order to describe the developmental arc that practice leaders went through as they established their positions and approaches to improving practice, we now need to concentrate on the qualitative data collected from the case studies of 30 settings. Around 40 practice leaders at different points of their careers were working and developing as leaders in these settings. (The number varied slightly during the course of the research due to career changes.) Over the three years that they were interviewed and observed and the quality of their settings was assessed for the research, they discussed their own development and how their professional identities and leadership interacted. Table 3.3 summarises the key areas of practice on which they led during the research period, any changes to their leadership roles, and the key mediating and moderating factors that had affected their ability to bring about improvements in their settings. The totals in Table 3.3 are derived from a total sample of around 40 EYP practice leaders who during the research could be involved in leading multiple activities within these categories.

The interviews highlighted a wide range of areas in which practice leaders were taking a lead, which we categorised according to the EYPS standards.[10]

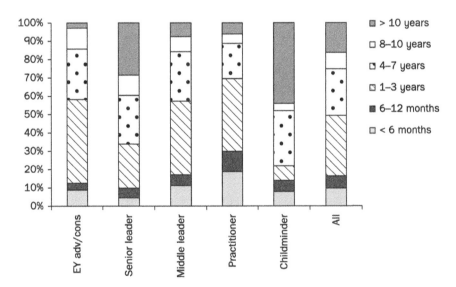

Figure 3.3 Time in current role (responses = 1,645).

Table 3.3 Key areas of practice leaders' activities

Knowledge	Practice	Partnership with families	Teamwork and collaboration	Relationships with children	Professional development	Leadership role	Leading change Mediating factors	Moderating factors
Disseminating new knowledge to staff (n = 8)	Balance between child- and adult-initiated (n = 12)	Well being and development (n = 10)	Culture of collaboration (n = 24)	Developing positive values and expectations (n = 8)	Mentoring and supporting others (n = 14)	Changes in areas of responsibility (n = 21)	Collective engagement in change (n = 21)	Staff resistance (n = 17)
Understanding of child development (n = 2)	Linking observation to planning and curriculum (n = 11)	Constructive relationships (n = 10)	Colleagues' roles (n = 7)	Better staff interaction with children (n = 5)	Running formal training (n = 13)	Changes to leadership structure (n = 9)	Good staff relationships (n = 12)	Lack of time (n = 12)
Increasing knowledge of EYFS (n = 4)	Improving quality of provision and environment (n = 10)	Develop outcomes (n = 7)	Influencing policy and practice (n = 5)	Child-to-child communication (n = 3)	Leading CPD (n = 13)	Changes to approach to leadership (n = 5)	Opportunities to implement gradually (n = 10)	Lack of resources (n = 9)
How to lead and support others (n = 3)	EYFS curriculum planning (n = 8)				Modelling practice (n = 10)		Support from outside (n = 7)	Workload (n = 8)
	Leading planning (n = 5)				Supporting staff to reflect on and evaluate practice (n = 10)			
	Outdoor play (n = 4)				Building learning community (n = 10)			
	Assessment (n = 3)				EYP network (n = 10)			
					Appraisal (n = 5)			

We added the two categories on the right of Table 3.3. The first, leadership role, captured changes to their leadership responsibilities, mainly reflecting movements in their position in their settings' leadership and management structures. The second category was concerned with their experience of leading change, specifically those factors that had supported their efforts to introduce improvements, which we termed mediating factors, and those that had inhibited their efforts, moderating factors.

This overview reflects these practice leaders' high levels of engagement in different aspects of professional development, They placed as much emphasis on informal development approaches, such as modelling best practice, as on the leadership of more formal professional development sessions, as one practice leader emphasised: '*I am very conscious that I am modelling [interactions] for staff as well as for children and parents.*' A great deal of this modelling was associated with improving practitioner–children interactions in key areas such as promoting sustained shared thinking or adopting more responsive pedagogical approaches.

It was in the area of professional development that they most often articulated their leadership and broad, and sometimes holistic, views of what they wished to achieve by:

> *Bringing together aspects of the role, e.g. feeding information back, mentoring and supporting other professionals in their role [. . .] developing policies together [. . .] more opportunities to model learning from courses, more mentoring/leading practice in distinct areas such as QA [quality assurance] policies.*
>
> (Practice leader, LS19)

There were a number of specific areas of practice where they had consistently been given, or had taken, leadership responsibility:

- Balancing child- and adult-initiated experiences
- Linking observation of children to planning and curriculum delivery
- Developing better relationships with parents.

In some cases, practice leaders were trying to develop all three simultaneously:

> *[We're] currently changing the planning for the children so it's more based on the child, using the child as starting-point rather than child development. We have been trialling this over the last five weeks, so the setting is in the middle of the change process. Previously, staff got together and chose a theme for the term, but not all the children wanted to take part. Now, themes are based on child*

observations with a lot of different themes going on at the same time. Following reorganisation of planning, child concentration has improved and children seem more settled.

(Practice leader, LS09)

Taking into account the range of areas practice leaders were responsible for, it is perhaps unsurprising that one of the most frequent developments they discussed was change in the scope of their leadership responsibilities. While discussion of changes in leadership approaches was less common, they were most frequently mentioned by more experienced leaders:

In the past I've always said I'm the boss and you will do as I say, but now I want staff to be on board and be happy with what they are doing. This has come from sharing practice with other professionals. We discuss different scenarios and how we have handled it differently. I used to make changes and get the credit for it. Now I see it as a team initiative and the team is the most important thing. I want morale to be up and for everyone to enjoy coming to work [. . .] I like to delegate responsibility. I also try to lead by example and model effective behaviour.

(Practice leader, LS13)

The interviews started to build a picture of the different types of dynamics that shaped practitioners' developing views of practice leadership and their identities as practice leaders. The framework that emerged from the analysis was based on three overlapping stages we termed 'Becoming', 'Being' and 'Developing':

- **Becoming.** This relates to the period during which many practitioners undertaking EYPS were still relatively new to seeing themselves – and being seen by others – as a practice leader. Here, the dynamic that started to affect their identities was mainly initiated by the impact of this training on their confidence, skills and current knowledge and understanding and therefore largely related to them as individuals. Generally, the less experienced the practitioner, the more extensive were the perceived impacts on professional identity.
- **Being.** This covers the period during which an individual becomes established and recognised as being a practice leader in her or his setting(s) by managers, colleagues and the wider professional network. The dynamics that most affected their professional identity at this stage were more social in nature than in the previous stage, as the practices they were engaged in led to them being recognised in their settings as leaders.

- **Developing.** Once recognised as leaders in their setting(s) or wider professional contexts, these leaders often took on new responsibilities and interacted with new groups of people. As a result, their sense of professional identity continued to develop, especially if they felt supported or 'liberated' to take on new roles and responsibilities and engage in new professional relationships. The dynamic here was still social in nature but more focused on their acceptance by other leaders, both in their setting(s) and their wider professional contexts.

During each of these phases of a practice leader's developmental arc, different types of dynamics influenced the relationship between their growing identity as leaders and their agency in their settings. During the 'Becoming' phase, the key dynamics tended to be more personal in nature. For example, a renewed focus on practice that was more critical and reflective in nature challenged one experienced manager's understanding of her practice, and hence the professional identity she derived from it:

> *I reflect on my own effectiveness more and my approach. I am able to focus on what is and isn't important [. . .] I think more about my sessions, reflective practice. The structure of a session, evaluation, has more emphasis. I probably would have done the same activity before EYPS but now I get more out of it through developing my skills of reflection. EYP training gets you to think of little things. You start to examine your everyday practice and question whether it is the most effective or not.*
>
> (LS12)

Increased levels of reflection and criticality were not only applied to existing practice, but also to notions of what constituted effective practice, as the following practice leader underlined:

> *We have always tried to build on children's interests. I personally have a better understanding of the EYFS and the research that has gone on beforehand. That affects the planning, everything. Now there is a distinct adult-led portion of the sessions and a distinct child-led portion where adults support the children's play. We try to avoid disrupting children's play. Adult-led activities are planned around observations of children's interests.*
>
> (LS06)

In the 'Being' phase, the key dynamics were more social and organisational, specifically the extent to which their leadership was recognised by others in the setting. If they were recognised, this encouraged practitioners to take on new responsibilities, adopt new practices, and change their relationships with colleagues, all of which influenced their professional identities as leaders:

> *I think it has changed. They see me more now as a leader rather than a manager. Previously I was like, 'We need to meet these outcomes as soon as possible' and it does not work because people get frustrated. Yes, we do need to implement stuff from the Government or the Education Department, but we need to do it in a way which suits us here, where everybody is involved. I think this works for us now much better.*

(LS49)

The dynamic in the 'Developing' phase was still social in nature but focused on these practice leaders being recognised and supported by other leaders. In this stage, as they often needed to learn about new areas of responsibility and how to implement ideas and innovations, their relationship to the formal and informal leadership structures, specifically the degree to which they 'liberated' their leadership, was key. One practice leader recalled how being appointed to her setting's senior management team led to her being recognised as a 'change agent' across the setting by colleagues. Another part of this dynamic in the Developing phase was broadening their professional networks as they progressed as a practice leader through mechanisms such as local EYP networks or meeting like-minded individuals facing similar challenges informally:

> *For me what the EYP role has definitely done is open up far more opportunities for networking and training to consolidate and support and scaffold my learning and what I am doing in the group. There are benefits of having a safe space outside in the EYP network to either let off steam or discuss problems and issues. The network is for sharing and pooling good practice.*

(LS19)

In summary, we used the notion that individuals progressed through the stages of 'Becoming, Being and Developing' to try and capture the nature of their development as leaders as they established themselves as practice leaders. This is best interpreted less as a linear progression through a series of distinct stages and more as a series of oscillations between professional growth and social recognition, initiated by different types of dynamics between their identity and agency as leaders.

Building practice leadership capacity

The role taken by practice leaders in developing the leadership capacity of their setting(s) depended in part on where they were on this development arc. It was also affected by the existing capacity of their settings. In some settings with high levels of capacity, individual practice leaders might receive as much support as they provided to others and be one of many practitioners offering advice and guidance, whereas in low capacity settings they might be the only source of support on offer to colleagues. The idea that a key responsibility of a leader in any organisation is to develop the leadership of others is a well-established aspect of leadership theory and practice and has evolved considerably in recent times. The relatively narrow notion of succession management has been expanded so that building leadership capacity is seen as a significant contributory factor to improving quality, a development that has run in parallel with increased interest in more distributed or hybrid forms of leadership.[11] Put simply, if leadership is seen as one of the most significant factors in improving the quality of provision in educational contexts,[12] having more of 'it' in any given context may work to accelerate and deepen the impact of any improvement efforts.

The notion that leadership is a social phenomenon, rather than a purely individual one, is supported by the growing number of studies of its effectiveness. Leadership research has moved on from the study of individuals and adopted a broader lens that focuses on individuals' positions in networks of leadership relationships (Resnick, 2010)[13] and to a consideration of leadership as a social act that arises from, and is stretched across, such networks (Spillane et al., 2004).[14]

Treating leadership capacity as a form of networked social capital meant that we placed importance on studying the professional communities and social networks in the settings.[15] We therefore needed not just to look at practice leaders as individual 'leaders', but also to analyse their impact on the communities or networks in which they are engaged in order to explore their role in building sufficient practice leadership capacity to improve the quality of provision in their settings.

How, then, did practice leaders develop the overall capacity for practice leadership in their settings? The two key findings from the research were that:

- Practice leaders needed to lead at multiple levels in a setting to build a sense of collective agency that united individuals, teams and the whole organisation.
- Practice leaders needed to align and cohere existing capacity by creating interconnections between individuals and groups, drawing on both informal professional networks and formal leadership structures.

Leading at multiple levels

There is a well-established tradition in leadership research of looking at multiple levels of leadership.[16] From this perspective of nested leadership, understanding the interactions between its different levels is a prerequisite to studying the leadership activities and effectiveness of specific leaders at each level. A similar approach was required to study how individual practice leaders built capacity, as the survey data indicated that they held different positions in the leadership hierarchies in their settings. Our study of their leadership was informed by the three broad levels of capacity building used by Hannah and Lester[17] in their model of professional learning:

- *Micro*: practice leadership is focused on colleagues' individual learning and practice and on affecting their beliefs and values.
- *Meso*: practice leadership is focused on groups, teams and social networks. It aims to improve the exchange of knowledge and practice while also affecting group norms and interactions.
- *Macro*: practice leadership is focused on developing and institutionalising practice leadership in management and CPD structures. It may also be outward looking for new and emergent practices and knowledge.

What types of activities were practice leaders engaged in at each of these different levels? A good starting point for identifying these were the most commonly cited mediating and moderating factors associated with leading change, collected in Table 3.3 above.

The most commonly cited mediating factor was 'collective engagement in developing the change'. In most instances, collective engagement was characterised by fairly general references to activities at the micro level such as discussing changes to planning outdoor play with colleagues (LS04); practice leaders' facilitating team work (LS53) or involving all staff in decisions about a change (LS20). In some settings, practice leaders spoke in more detail of how they had changed their practice to build collective engagement at the meso level, for example by working incrementally with key, small groups of staff to overcome resistance through deciding to *'focus on one area of change jointly and [. . .] allocate responsibilities within that'* (LS06). In other settings, practice leaders were working at a macro level as they introduced a formal mentoring scheme to reduce the leadership hierarchy (LS12), extended consultation with staff for parents and children about changes to the outdoor environment (LS18; LS49), or used a manager's prolonged absence to introduce more delegation to the setting in general (LS24).

Collective working at all levels was used to develop leadership capacity by building joint ownership of improvement efforts, and a common language around them, in order to make it easier to build consensus among other practitioners about the need for change (LS29; LS59). As one practice leader underlined: *'Always consider somebody else first – doing the personal, team bit first. Part of that is trying to encourage them to come round to your way of thinking'* (LS28).

Reflecting the survey data, the most commonly cited moderating factor was staff resistance to change. Beyond a general, unspecified reluctance to change, the origins of this resistance encompassed a range of specific factors. They included initiative overload and the sheer pace of change in early years (LS20; LS24), staff instability and the difficulty of mobilising a part-time workforce for training or collective discussion (LS24; LS51), and the complexity of having to build relationships with a range of practitioners for leaders who operated across multiple settings (LS01; LS17). Practice leaders attempted to overcome resistance in a number of ways, many of which have already been discussed, notably breaking changes down into small steps for staff and building consensus around the need for improvement: *'we try to get them involved from the very first stage to help with their resistance as much as we possibly can'* (LS49).

Every practice leader was interviewed for the case studies about their activities at each level using a framework adapted from previous research into early years leadership.[18] We adapted the framework so that, rather than searching for generic characteristics of effective leaders, we focused on their leadership of improvements in practice. The outcomes of these interviews illustrated the causal accounts that were woven through the case studies, and form a major section of each case report, examples of which have been included in the case studies in Chapter 5. The seven areas considered across the differing levels of practice leaders' activity (macro, meso, micro) were as follows:

1 **Visioning** – identifying and articulating a shared vision of specific aspects of pedagogy, the curriculum and notions of quality.
2 **Developing shared understanding** – of the rationale and importance of key practices, processes and outcomes.
3 **Communication with colleagues** – setting out clear expectations in terms of quality of practice and roles. Challenging existing norms and expectations.
4 **Promoting effective learning relationships** – and building supportive networks and communities by improving colleagues' sense of themselves as learners and practice leaders.
5 **Engagement in ongoing professional development** – involving other staff in a range of professional development experiences – both

formal and informal – focused on the core issues of early years pedagogy and improvement to the quality of provision.

6   **Monitoring, assessing and innovating** – using a range of processes to provide feedback on performance to colleagues, assess the quality of provision and interactions and ensure they are fed back into changes in practice and planning processes. In some cases, explicit mechanisms and processes are used to implement changes and evaluate impact (e.g. action research).

7   **Encouraging and facilitating parent and community partnerships** – improving understanding of home and setting approaches to pedagogy, developing greater consistency of approaches, and working in partnership with parents to develop the quality of their interactions with children.

Applying these notions of effective leadership to the different levels, particularly the micro interactions between staff, highlighted subtle differences in how each was enacted, while reinforcing the applicability of these constructs to all levels of leadership. It also highlighted a much more important issue. Often in studies of leadership, particularly those that focus on individual senior leaders and their broad organisational impacts, key leadership practices, such as visioning, become wrapped up with their individual agency, their ability to articulate a strategic vision that they can convince others to accept, rather than with developing a sense of collective agency. In constructing these accounts of practice leaders, the closeness of most leaders to practice, and therefore to their colleagues and children, allowed a more collective notion of the type of agency required to bring about improvement to be developed. In the following vignette, this notion of collective agency comes through, along with a particular notion of 'visioning' when enacted at the micro and meso levels of leaderships.

Vignette 1: Improving adult–child interaction collectively

In this vignette, a practice leader working in a fairly small voluntary setting (LS06) discusses the development of a new 'vision' for adult–child interactions. This vision, informed by her experience of EYPS and the recommendations of the EYFS, focused on increasing the proportion of child-initiated activities in the setting.

Louise's main responsibilities in the setting were to plan and organise activities for the children, manage staffing and staff meetings, staff appraisals and support for staff in general. Improving interactions between staff and children was a key improvement priority during the research. During the first visit, her focus was on the importance of listening and responding to children:

I am role modelling listening to children and standing back and observing. The interactions form the basis of our planning. Planning has developed through Foundation Degree, EYPS and EYFS changes. We always have at least an hour's child-initiated play. Enhancement of the room is through what the children have demonstrated an interest in. We have developed children's learning through their own activities and sometimes their own mistakes. Adults are supporting children and scaffolding their learning. Ongoing review of learning journey books with children also informs planning and guides children's thinking.

Louise also felt at that time that interaction around children's play was a key issue and was acutely aware of the need to introduce changes gradually:

We have always been battling with getting the balance right between adult-led and child-initiated learning. Since I have done my Foundation Degree, all the extra training and EYP, it's given me the thought process [and] I have a better understanding. It's not such a battle anymore. We can see when we have got the balance right. It's having that confidence yourself to say, 'Yes, we feel it's right, the children are happy.'

Louise's vision of the kinds of interactions she wanted to see were shaped in part by EYFS guidance and the inspection frameworks, but she also attributed her strongly held views to professional values about how others should be treated. In fact, she had been strongly influenced by a childminder whose relationships with adults and children she particularly admired. Like many other practice leaders, she had been emboldened to introduce changes by the learning and confidence she derived from gaining EYPS, as she emphasised during one of the later visits: '*For me it started off having a better understanding about why that balance is important so that it isn't mostly adult-led because the children can show exactly what they know in child-initiated play.*'

Louise used a range of micro and meso leadership practices to implement the vision she had developed: '*I know staff watch me and change their practices through watching me.*' In weekly team meetings, all staff were encouraged to be proactive about introducing new ideas and receptive to innovations: '*Weekly meetings are a major place for developing change but it is a forum for all staff to use.*' She also gave staff readings to help them understand the importance of effective pedagogical interaction. Louise recognised that there were differences of interpretation and that people observed children in different ways but viewed these as a strength, as it was likely to support a range of learning approaches: '*It is a mature staff and I trust if they say to me I've got to do that with my key group then I support them. It works both ways.*' Interviews with staff strongly correlated Louise's comments. One of her colleagues reflected on the process they had gone through during the research period:

> *Previously we were all very hung up on ensuring adult-led learning was done. Through the training we were getting and reflection we became more comfortable with trusting our own good practice and instincts and we realised we didn't need to spend all that time on adult-led learning. We could get the same things from child-initiated activity [. . .] We didn't realise we were doing those things and the importance of it. Through discussions, staff meetings and training, through written observations and evaluations, we could see the quality of what we were doing.*

She also drew attention to the importance of the induction process which Louise had established: '*Induction did touch on interaction specifically*', and new members of staff were encouraged to watch and learn from other members of staff, as another practitioner commented: '*I just get the vibe that it is more child-initiated here than my previous setting.*' Louise was consistently identified as the primary role model and source of information but, as practice leadership capacity in the setting grew, new practitioners increasingly took a lead from other members of staff and how they did things. Over time informal discussions of activities provided an opportunity to reinforce the now established vision for effective interactions in the setting, as another staff member outlined:

> *We go from the child's interests. That's what we're taught and that's what we practise until there is no direction anymore [. . .] I think there is just a very sensitive spot where the adult needs to intervene and then just gently change [the child's] route without completely disregarding them.*

When asked who influenced this practice, she responded: '*Louise – she's really acute at finding that spot and emphasises that sensitive balance between child-led and adult-initiated play.*'

It is relatively easily to identify in this short vignette examples of Louise's practice leadership at all three levels and across most of the key areas of leadership, from modelling the interactions herself to setting up a new induction process for all new staff to ensure that they were clear about how the setting operated. Just as important as the notion of leading at multiple levels in the setting was the sense of collective agency, a cornerstone of building leadership capacity. Collective agency, defined as the ability of a group to act together in order to effect change, requires a shared sense of purpose, a rationale that is inclusive and persuasive and leaders who are happy to share their influence and adopt more distributed forms of leadership. This vignette provides a good introduction to the next section, which explores the role of practice leaders in aligning and cohering existing capacity by helping to make connections among different groups and individuals.

Aligning and cohering existing capacity

In order to understand the practice leader's position in the formal leadership structures and to help us reconstruct their interactions with colleagues, we constructed an organogram of each setting. Figure 3.4 is the leadership structure for a setting (LS28) made up of a group of three nurseries in the East Midlands. This setting is also the focus of case study 3 in Chapter 5.

Studying formal leadership structures can only provide a partial account of practice leaders' attempts to cohere and connect the capacity of individuals and teams in their settings. This is because, beyond these formal structures, they are also members of networks and communities, both inside and outside of the setting, which they use to improve practice. The causal logic that links

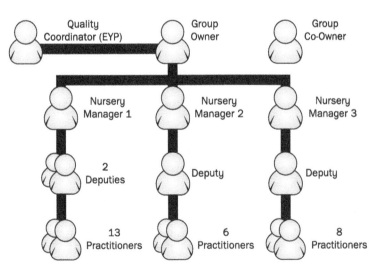

Figure 3.4 Formal leadership structure (LS28).

individual leaders, professional networks and communities and capacity building is as follows:

- individuals can receive a range of **support from new knowledge to emotional help** from the professional community that surrounds them;
- these communities can create **contexts that enable individuals to make changes** in their practice by providing trusting relationships and developing cultures of risk taking;
- changes in practice in turn develop **new understandings and norms** that re-shape, and re-contextualise, the community and increase its ability to support further change.

Practice leaders can therefore either draw on these networks to support themselves or be involved in building them in order to support others to make changes. It is the latter process of building professional networks in settings that is the focus of this section. The conceptual link between individual practice leaders, their professional networks and the development of collective capacity is social capital. This is the notion that beyond individuals' personal capacities, or human capital, they can use their relationships and networks to access varying degrees of social capital, the resources held collectively in a social network, to help them achieve their aims. As well as draw down social capital to achieve their own ends, leaders can also use their positions to re-direct it to others in the community. The social capital an individual can draw down will therefore vary depending on their position in a network or setting, the people in the network, and the quality and depth of their interrelationships. Practice leaders can influence individual and collective agency by building professional networks and communities that provide support, give access to new knowledge and create a culture of trust and risk taking.

To research the development of practice leadership capacity in professional networks, we used a specific form of social network analysis (SNA) that focused on where practice leaders were positioned in the social networks in the setting. The SNA provided a picture of how individuals in the setting interacted with each other and who they went to for advice and support, and it allowed us to create a series of sociograms that illustrated how these relationships changed over time, thus providing a real-time analysis of the development of the professional networks and communities in the settings. These sociograms provided a means of assessing the extent to which the practice leaders had developed viable professional communities, or supportive professional networks, in settings.

To understand the link between individual and collective agency in the settings, we had to differentiate in the SNA analysis and other data collection activities between those leadership activities that were more concerned with developing and sustaining the viability of the community or network and those that were more concerned with supporting changes in individual practices.[19] We needed to track the development of these networks over time and link them to specific practice changes. To illustrate the potential impact of these professional networks on settings' improvement journey, the following vignette describes two very different settings: one in which a highly connected network developed that supported practice leaders at all levels and a second case where such a network was not formed.

Vignette 2: A tale of two practice leaders

The two practice leaders we compare in this extended vignette are Georgina, who was a Children's Centre Teacher working across two children's centres in inner city Birmingham (LS01), and Nena, a Lead Practitioner in a voluntary setting in North London (LS49). The children's centre in Birmingham, which was the focus of the research, had around 45 children on roll and 13 members of staff during the period of the research. The nursery in London, which is also the focus of case study 1 in Chapter 5, had around 60 children on roll and around 24 members of staff. As Figures 3.5 and 3.6 indicate, the formal leadership structures of the two settings were similar. The children's centre was slightly more hierarchical, with Georgina operating as part of the senior

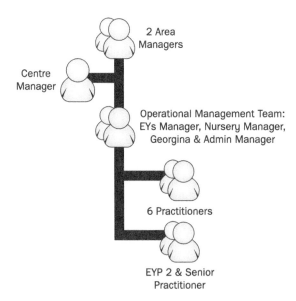

Figure 3.5 Formal leadership structure (LS01).

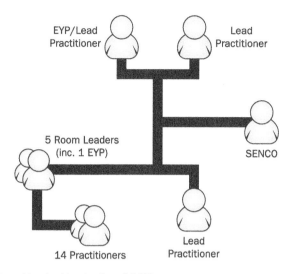

EYP/Lead Practitioner

Lead Practitioner

5 Room Leaders (inc. 1 EYP)

SENCO

14 Practitioners

Lead Practitioner

Figure 3.6 Formal leadership structure (LS49).

management team, below a centre manager and above two tiers of practitioners.

The nursery in London had a flatter structure, with Nena (EYP/Lead Practitioner in Figure 3.6) leading as one of two lead practitioners (a third joined the setting at the end of the research), above room leaders and practitioners. The lead practitioner role was introduced at the beginning of the research period as part of an explicit strategy to share the setting's leadership. Nena's role was to lead practice, while her fellow lead practitioner, who had previously been the setting's manager, focused on administration and working with parents. In this respect, Nena's and Georgina's responsibilities in relation to practice were fairly similar.

The SNA differentiated between the levels of support on offer to practitioners in settings, ranging from whom they might talk to about work-related issues or go to for ideas about improving practice, to asking about whose help had substantially changed how they developed children's learning in the preceding 12 months. They were also asked about who they had gone to for advice and support about a specific innovation in the setting being led by the practice leader. Undertaken three times during the research, the SNA allowed us to trace how informal professional networks in settings functioned and developed.

The following sociograms were created by drawing a line between practitioners and up to three people to whom they had gone for support or advice on various issues. The more lines there are connecting individuals, the closer and tighter knit the network. The more lines attached to an individual, the more frequently they are sought out for advice and support; and the more connected they are to others, the more central they are in the network.

If we begin by concentrating on Georgina in Figure 3.7, we find someone who initially tends to be on the edge of a small network of senior and middle leaders. As the research progressed, Georgina became more central as her network connections increased. However, as Figure 3.8 underlines, the centre's

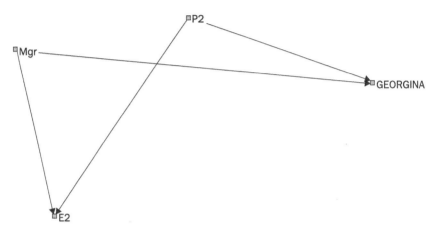

Figure 3.7 Sources of new ideas about improving practice in the setting (LSO1, SNA survey 1).

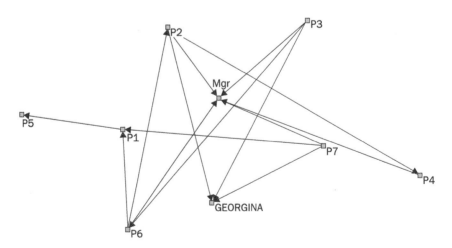

Figure 3.8 Sources of new ideas about improving practice in the setting (LSO1, SNA survey 3).

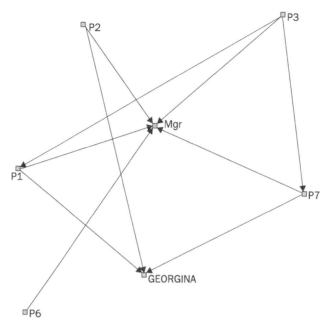

Figure 3.9 Sources of advice or support that had substantively changed how staff developed children's learning (LS01, SNA survey 3).

manager remained the hub of a relatively closed network when it came to seeking out new ideas about improving practice.

A similar pattern was apparent when staff in the setting were asked who had changed their approach to children's learning in the previous 12 months (Figure 3.9). It was only when staff were asked about whom they had sought advice and support from with regard to a specific innovation led by Georgina that she emerged as more central to the network, with more connections than the setting's manager, as Figure 3.10 illustrates.

In contrast, Nena was very much at the centre of an extensive network from the beginning of the research. She was one of three people, together with the manager and one of the five room leaders at this point, who functioned as a hub for over half the staff in the setting (see Figure 3.11).

Within a year, the innovation network had developed further. Nena and the other lead practitioner remained at the centre but a more distributed set of connections was starting to emerge as more of the room leaders were being seen as sources of innovation by the other practitioners. This can be seen in Figure 3.12 in the series of mini-hubs that had emerged around two of the room leaders (RL1 and RL2) and the setting's family support coordinator.

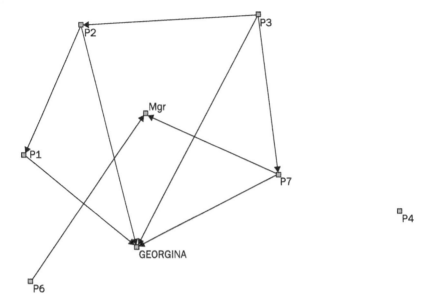

Figure 3.10 Sources of advice or support about the change led by Georgina (LS01, SNA survey 3).

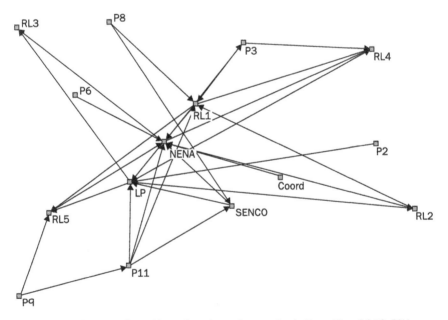

Figure 3.11 Sources of new ideas about improving practice in the setting (LS49, SNA survey 1).

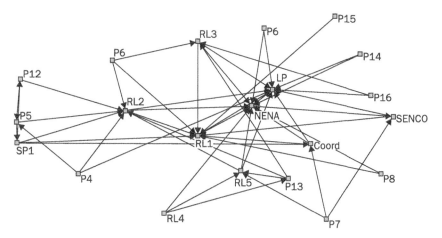

Figure 3.12 Sources of new ideas about improving practice in the setting (LS49, SNA survey 2).

This pattern of emergent hubs was even more pronounced when we looked at the networks of support that had substantially changed practitioners' approach to learning during the preceding 12 months. Figure 3.13 shows Nena, the other leader practitioner and room leader 1 as part of a linked hub that came close to replicating the formal leadership structure of the setting.

Seventeen months later, the setting's capacity for practice leadership had grown, and a very different network, depicted in Figure 3.14, had emerged in which a number of the room leaders were much more engaged in the network as mini-hubs of support and advice.

By the end of the research, there was a much denser and decentralised web of interconnections in the setting. While Nena and the other lead practitioner remained relatively central, other mini-hubs had started to emerge. What is also interesting about this network pattern is that it was relatively stable across different areas of support and advice, whether it related to developing children's social and emotional wellbeing or to offering general support. This contrasts with many of the other settings in which the professional networks tended to vary according to the nature of support and advice being sought. Most surprisingly, the pattern remains relatively stable in relation to the initiative led by Nena, which gives a very strong indication of how successful she and the other lead practitioner had been in developing a more networked or distributed approach to leading practice innovation, as Figure 3.15 indicates.

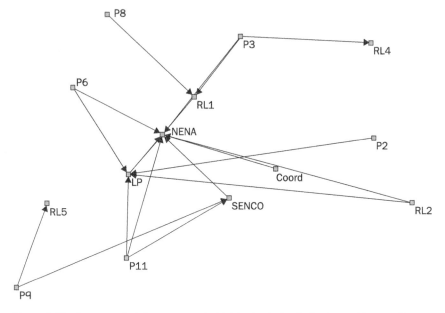

Figure 3.13 Sources of advice or support which had substantively changed how staff developed children's learning (LS49, SNA survey 1).

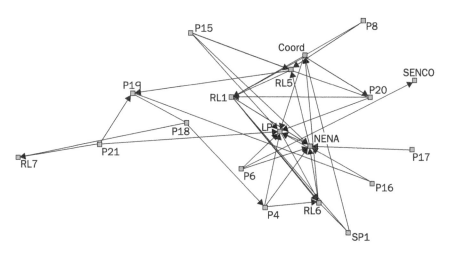

Figure 3.14 Sources of advice or support which had substantively changed how staff developed children's learning in the previous 12 months (LS49, SNA survey 3).

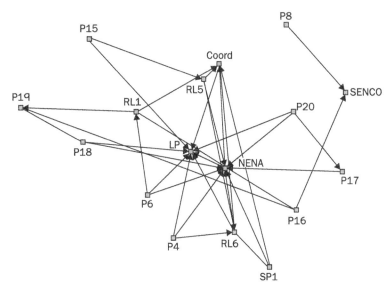

Figure 3.15   Sources of advice or support about the change led by Nena in the last 12 months (LS49, SNA survey 3).

Explaining the variations

What, then, happened in these two settings to account for the changes in what we observed? In the children's centre, we found a relatively closed network with limited connections in which Georgina struggled to make herself central. Indeed, the only point at which she seemed to achieve this was when she was directly leading the innovation that was the focus of the network. In contrast, Nena was central to all the professional networks, whose hubs were very similar to the setting's formal leadership structure. Over time in her setting, the networks became increasingly dense with far more connections between staff and a number of mini-hubs emerging, based around more of the room leaders taking practice leadership roles in providing support and advice to others. Although Nena remained central to all the networks, she was increasingly less critical to practice innovation as new leaders were emerging throughout the setting, particularly at lower levels of the formal leadership structure, as the result of their improvement strategy. You can find a more detailed account of Nena's setting in the first case study of Chapter 5, so here we concentrate on contrasting the capacity-building approaches in the two settings.

At the beginning of the study, Georgina was not line managed by anyone and the centre manager was happy for her to decide on priorities and change foci: '*If [Georgina] identified it and "owns" it, it was natural to let her take the lead on it.*' However, Georgina sometimes felt '*isolated because I'm not in a school or a nursery with other education professionals*'. To counter this, she closely monitored government and local policy guidelines and initiatives relating to early years and was very much self-directing in her developing practice leadership role. However, as a result the nature and scope of Georgina's leadership practice had become predominantly strategic by the end of the research and had led to what she described as '*a dramatic reduction in the time spent in nursery*'. By the middle of the research, Georgina felt that her time spent with the children had progressively reduced since taking on her position. While she oversaw the curriculum, learning environment planning and assessment across the setting, Georgina did not manage staff beyond leading CPD if it related to an area that she oversaw. Towards the end of the study, she spent an increasing amount of time out of the nursery, undertaking tasks such as setting up new strands of nursery provision, pursuing grant applications and monitoring new early years initiatives. Georgina's practice leadership was predominantly focused at the macro level, on improving practitioners' exchanges of knowledge and shaping group norms and interactions. She also consistently looked for new and emergent practices, guidance and knowledge to use as drivers for change. For example, a visit to another children's centre inspired Georgina to adapt her own centre's process for tracking children's progress.

As a consequence, Georgina's direct impact on children's outcomes was moderated by structural leadership factors that reduced opportunities for her to work directly with practitioners and children. Her description of this revealed the tensions she was attempting to reconcile: '*I've been involved in the centre more strategically rather than just doing my job at the moment.*' She felt this had a negative impact on the degree to which changes were managed effectively. Asked how she overcame this, she replied that, depending on the change, she sometimes allowed staff the autonomy to cease its implementation if they did not feel it was working: '*You get better and better at letting go and actually the things that are really working, staff will keep won't they? If they've tried things and it's not making a difference, then they'll ditch that.*'

Staff were expected to liaise with Georgina and discuss with her why changes were unsuitable. She would also consult with the centre's manager and senior practitioner. However, her absence from the nursery restricted opportunities for her to model practice and offer support and guidance to staff in developing, implementing and reviewing change. This resulted in changes not being sustained, which increasingly frustrated her: '*I think I have been more of that "seagull" who drops something and then you're up again, which is not very good.*'

In contrast, Nena's redesignation, after gaining EYPS, as one of two 'lead practitioners' in the setting, along with the setting's manager, signalled an explicit shift towards them both working on a more equal basis with practitioners. Nena's primary focus was on training and mentoring colleagues, as well as working directly with children and maintaining and updating policies. As the case study in Chapter 5 explains in detail, the empowerment of room leaders was the main focus of improvement in the setting during the course of the research. To support the emergent practice leadership of the room leaders, Nena developed a programme of leadership workshops, drawing on her own training, that she delivered in the setting, designed to support room leaders to take responsibility for improving practice in their rooms.

In terms of building capacity, the settings could hardly have been more different. Georgina's role was restricted to one level of leadership: the macro or strategic. Her approach to innovations was restricted by her inability to work directly with staff at other levels to help them to introduce the new ideas she brought in from her horizon scanning. Even though she led formal professional development activities in key areas, the limited practice leadership capacity in the setting meant that she found it difficult to sustain certain innovations. Georgina recognised this as an issue, and became frustrated by it: her peripheral positions in the setting's professional networks meant that she had limited opportunities to change the situation. On the other hand, the shift in emphasis associated with Nena's position as lead required her to work at the meso and micro levels much more than previously. Initially, she was at the centre of a series of professional networks that largely mirrored the formal leadership structure. This allowed her to have a sustained influence on the room leaders they wanted to take on greater practice leadership responsibility. Through training and connecting room leaders more closely to other staff members, Nena and her colleague lead practitioner generated greater capacity in individual rooms and in the setting as a whole. To some extent, this whole approach was prompted by the recognition that high staff turnover, which can severely reduce a setting's capacity, was having a negative effect on the quality of provision. One of the key benefits of a densely connected professional network is the amount of built-in redundancy it has. This means that the loss of one or two individuals is less problematic because practitioners remain connected to others who can continue to offer support and advice.

Summary

In summary, the contrast between the approaches adopted by these two practice leaders in developing the quality of provision is striking. It also reflects the wider findings of the research, in that the settings that failed to improve the overall quality of their practice during the research period tended to be those where practice leaders were unable to overcome the following barriers:

- They were not recognised by the formal leadership or given the authority to lead at different levels. As a result, they often spent very little time working directly with colleagues and children: '*She does not manage or lead individuals. Her leadership role involves a lot of the admin responsibilities, which are delegated to her because of her background in finance. Her leadership is more on the administrative side and less about the development of others' pedagogy*' (extract from LS24 case report).

- They were either unable to support staff in accessing professional development or failed to sustain sufficiently high levels of involvement: '*This is where we kind of struggle sometimes because some of the things people expect [other staff] to get involved with I take on because I get paid extra to do it. I get paid my admin hours whereas they don't, so anything they do would have to be done voluntarily which isn't fair and we don't have time during the session and are always on maximum numbers with the staff we have got and even when we've got children with additional needs in it's manic*' (LS15 case report).

- They struggled to encourage other practitioners, who often lacked confidence and had low levels of qualifications, to take risks and innovate: '*In this nursery it is very receptive to change. They take it on board. They are very enthusiastic, the staff here. But [in] the other nursery the workforce is very different, lots of them entrenched in old styles, many of them were trained a long time ago. You find it takes a lot longer to get through there than it does here*' (LS14 case report)

In Chapter 4, we focus in detail on successful practice leadership in action, outlining how practice leaders overcome these barriers to improve the quality of provision in many settings. We also delineate the four main strands of practice leadership that emerged from the study in order to give you an impression of what practice leadership actually looked like in these settings and contexts.

Notes

1 Hadfield, M., Jopling, M., Royle, K. and Waller, T. (2011) *First National Survey of Practitioners with Early Years Professional Status*. London: CWDC; Hadfield, M. and Jopling, M. (2012) *Second National Survey of Practitioners with Early Years Professional Status Report*. Research Report DFE-RR239a. London: DfE.

2 See Hadfield and Jopling (2012).

3 See Britzman, D.P. (1992) Cultural myths in the making of a teacher: biography and social structure in teacher education, in M. Okazawa-Rey, J. Anderson

and R. Traver (eds.) *Teachers, Teaching, and Teacher Education*. Cambridge, MA: Harvard Education Review; Day, C., Kington, A., Stobart, G. and Sammons, P. (2006) The personal and professional selves of teachers: stable and unstable identities, *British Educational Research Journal*, 32 (4), 601–16.

4   See Adams, K. (2008) What's in a name? Seeking professional status through degree studies within the Scottish early years context, *European Early Education Research Journal*, 16 (2), 196–209; Lloyd, E. and Hallet, E. (2010) Professionalising the early childhood workforce in England: work in progress or missed opportunity?, *Contemporary Issues in Early Childhood*, 11 (1), 75–86; McGillivray, G. (2011) Constructions of professional identity, in L. Miller and C. Cable (eds.) *Professionalization, Leadership and Management in the Early Years*. London: Sage; Miller, L. (2008) Developing professionalism within a regulatory framework in England: challenges and possibilities, *European Early Childhood Education Research Journal*, 16 (2), 255–68; Murray, J. (2013) Becoming an early years professional: developing a new professional identity, *European Early Childhood Education Research Journal*, 21 (4), 527–40.

5   Miller (2008), at p. 266.

6   Miller (2008); Fenech, M. and Sumsion, J. (2007) Early childhood teachers and regulation: complicating power relations using a Foucauldian lens, *Contemporary Issues in Early Childhood*, 8 (2), 109–22.

7   McGillivray (2011), at p. 98.

8   Kuisma, M. and Sandberg, A. (2008) Preschool teachers' and student teachers' thoughts about professionalism in Sweden, *European Education Research Journal*, 16 (2), 186–95.

9   Hadfield and Jopling (2012).

10 Children's Workforce Development Council (CWDC) (2010) *On the Right Track: Guidance to the Standards for the Award of Early Years Professional Status*. Leeds: CWDC.

11 See Spillane, J., Halverson, R. and Diamond, J. (2004) Towards a theory of leadership practice: a distributed perspective, *Journal of Curriculum Studies*, 36 (1), 3–34; Gronn, P. (2011) Hybrid configurations of leadership, in A. Bryman, D. Collinson, K. Grint, B. Jackson and M. Uhl-Bien (eds.) *Sage Handbook of Leadership*. London: Sage.

12 Robinson, V., Hohepa, M. and Lloyd, C. (2009) *School Leadership and Student Outcomes: Identifying What Works and Why: Best Evidence Synthesis Iteration [BES]*. Wellington, NZ: Ministry of Education.

13 Resnick, L. (2010) Nested learning systems for the thinking curriculum, *Educational Researcher*, 39 (3), 183–97.

14 Spillane et al. (2004).

15 Coburn, C.E. and Russell, J.L. (2008) District policy and teachers' social networks, *Educational Evaluation and Policy Analysis*, 30 (3), 203–35; Daly,

A.J. and Finnigan, K. (2010) A bridge between worlds: understanding network structure to understand change strategy, *Journal of Educational Change*, 11 (2), 111–38.

16   See, for example, Yammarino, F.J., Dionne, S.D., Chun, J.U. and Dansereau, F. (2005) Leadership and levels of analysis: a state-of-the-science review, *The Leadership Quarterly*, 16 (6), 879–919; Resnick (2010).

17   Hannah, S. and Lester, P. (2009) A multilevel approach to building and leading learning organizations, *The Leadership Quarterly*, 20, 34–48.

18   Siraj-Blatchford, I. and Manni, L. (2007) *Effective Leadership in the Early Years Sector*. London: Institute of Education, University of London; Office for Standards in Education (Ofsted) (2008) *Early Years: Leading to Excellence*. London: Ofsted.

19   Balkundi, P. and Harrison, D.A. (2006) Ties, leaders, and time in teams: strong inference about the effects of network structure on team viability and performance, *Academy of Management Journal*, 49, 49–68.

PART 2

4 Practice leadership in action

In this chapter, we introduce a developmental model that is designed to illustrate practice leadership in action. It allows us to focus on what practice leaders actually *did* to improve quality and the extent to which the strategies and approaches they used varied depending on the settings' initial capacity for practice leadership and key leaders' ability to develop further practice leadership capacity to effect change. It is important to emphasise that this is a dynamic and interdependent process, which continuously requires leaders to adjust what they do as improvements take effect. Similarly, as practice leadership is distributed throughout a setting, it sets up a series of feedback loops that expand the practice leadership capacity available to support any element of change and, in the process, further develop capacity. This chapter illustrates what happens in the central link of the logic model outlined in Chapter 2, as emergent practice leadership capacity becomes established, then embedded, in action in settings.

The model we explore in this chapter provides an overview of the progress made by the case study settings during the course of the research and a framework for interpreting and integrating the case studies contained in Chapter 5. In this chapter, we also outline in detail the four main interdependent strands of practice leadership that emerged from our research, set in the context of the differing types and levels of leadership roles and responsibilities found in the settings. As Chapter 3 suggests, this has allowed us to begin to address the need highlighted in recent research into educational leadership in general to focus explicitly on *how* practice leadership was enacted and shared, rather than on adumbrating leaders' roles and responsibilities.[1]

As Figures 2.10 and 2.11 in Chapter 2 indicate, comparison of the baseline with the final assessments of quality in the settings, which drew on the data collected relating to framing pedagogies and pedagogical interactions and to key external measures such as Ofsted ratings, enabled us to categorise the settings into four categories for quality improvement:

1   Settings which improved significantly from a low quality baseline
2   Settings which maintained high quality throughout the research
3   Settings which remained static in terms of quality or changed little
4   Settings where quality was inconsistent.

All nine settings in category 1 made educationally significant improvements in their process quality, improvements which appeared to be largely the result of their focusing on improving pedagogical framing. The settings that improved most were those where practice leaders focused on improving both aspects of process quality: pedagogical framing *and* pedagogical interactions. Settings in categories 3 and 4 were less likely to have made significant improvements in either aspect. Settings in category 2 maintained high quality by focusing on both aspects of process quality.

These four broad quality improvement categories, into which all the settings were placed, provided the starting point for our analysis of practice leadership. This focused on identifying similarities and differences in practice leaders' improvement practices in and across the four categories. These practices were analysed using constructs drawn from Siraj-Blatchford and Manni's research on effective leadership in the early years and Hannah and Lester's work on leadership capacity building, as outlined in Chapter 3.[2] The use of social network analysis (SNA) allowed us also to map the flow of relationships between practice leaders and their colleagues and build up a picture of the professional communities in each setting. As the case studies in Chapter 5 indicate, by repeating the SNA over time, we were able to map the development of such communities in some cases and shifts in a practice leader's position in them.

From quality improvement to practice leadership approaches

The category 1 settings were the starting point for the analyses, as they had improved quality most significantly. A detailed analysis of their improvement profiles had already been completed to create the categories in the first place (see Figure 2.11). Through analysing practice leaders' activities, we were able to identify two groups of practice leaders. As already suggested, the first group was made up of leaders who had improved their settings' quality ratings, primarily through focusing on aspects of framing pedagogy in their setting(s). The second group contained those leaders who had made the most significant improvements in pedagogical interactions while also improving pedagogical framing. These settings achieved the most educationally significant improvements in quality in the study.

There were substantial overlaps between the two groups in terms of leadership practices employed, with more similarities than differences compared with Siraj-Blatchford and Manni's taxonomy of effective leadership characteristics and behaviour.[3] As we have already emphasised, the analysis indicated that it was more important to understand *how* practice leaders carried out these practices and which characteristics they were able to draw on and exploit in their particular contexts, than *what* they did, in order to clarify the relationship between their practice leadership and the settings' improvement trajectories. Key contextual factors ranged from the existing quality of provision, the resources to hand and the settings' size and nature, to the role practice leaders occupied in the setting and the extent to which they were able to lead, rather than focus on management or administration.

The main factors that shaped their leadership were the overall capacity for, and maturity of, practice leadership in the settings. This capacity encompassed two key factors: the extent to which practice leaders had developed an understanding of what constituted high quality interactions and framing pedagogies in the setting, and the degree to which improvement processes had been embedded in a culture which supported learning, innovation and risk taking. If understanding of and responsibility for improvements did not extend beyond the practice leader or small group of practice leaders, the gains in quality risked becoming fragile and temporary, as a practice leader in one of the category 2 settings explained:

> *The changes are embedded, but if I left it wouldn't continue, so this is where the delegation is needed [. . .] Without me looking at the learning, it would go back to that.*
>
> (Practice leader, LS13)

The two overall approaches to practice leadership identified in category 1 settings were related to differences in overall practice leadership capacity and were termed:

(a) **emergent**, in that practice leadership was not well developed and was thus restricted in scope in these settings. Leadership was still likely to be fairly 'top-down' in approach.
(b) **established**, in that a broader and more distributed notion of practice leadership had become established, even though it may have been restricted to an individual practice leader at that point.

We then applied our analysis to the group of settings that had maintained high quality throughout the study (category 2). Settings in this group began the study with high quality provision and were unable to demonstrate significant gains in their approach to pedagogical framing because their baseline scores were so high. Consequently, where educationally significant improvements did occur, it was in pedagogical interactions, particularly in the area of cognitive challenge. What distinguished practice leadership in settings in this category was the extent to which it had been integrated into formalised leadership structures, thus embedding a commitment to improving quality in terms of *both* pedagogical framing and interactions into the culture and ethos of the settings. This recognition led to the development of a third overall approach to practice leadership, which we termed:

(c) **embedded**, to indicate that practice leadership was recognised as a specific aspect of leadership in the setting and that substantial numbers of other practitioners were engaged in improving process quality. Thus, practice leadership was widely distributed, or 'hybrid' (Gronn, 2011),[4] incorporating elements of both top-down and bottom-up leadership.

Practice leaders defined their approach to leadership primarily in terms of improving the quality of pedagogical processes in their settings. This meant they focused on interactions between staff and children, planning, and the quality of the learning environment, and were heavily involved in providing support for other staff. In practice, they engaged in forms of pedagogical leadership in that they led improvements in the quality of pedagogical processes in settings and set out to inform and enhance others' pedagogical practices through a range of mechanisms. In the settings that made educationally significant improvements to the quality of their processes or sustained high levels of quality provision throughout the research, practice leaders focused on four key outcomes. We characterised these as follows:

• strategically assessing the quality of current provision and relating this to an overall vision of quality;
• establishing a common understanding of improvements that were required and developing norms around quality;
• developing, leading and evaluating professional development activities that focused on improving process quality;
• enhancing practice leadership capacity in the setting by connecting individuals and building teams.

These four outcomes represent practice leadership in action and in the rest of this chapter we explore them in detail. For each approach, we use settings at different positions of the quality improvement continuum to illustrate how practice leadership was enacted and to highlight the contextual factors that affected its development in the settings.

Strategically assessing the quality of the current provision and relating this to an overall vision of quality

Settings' and practice leaders' visions of quality were enacted in different ways and at varying levels. Some visions were explicitly defined and used to guide improvement; others were more developmental. All were refined in the light of the other outcomes discussed in this chapter, as common understandings of improvement were created, professional development was undertaken and practice leadership capacity was enhanced.

In the settings in which practice leadership was **embedded**, practice leaders' articulation of quality provision and how they used it to assess the development of their settings varied considerably, depending on their position in the formal leadership structure. The fact that they had established practice leadership roles allowed them to do this with greater scope and depth than those in less established roles. They also tended to be the more data-rich settings, which used a number of external frameworks and perspectives to reflect on their practice and the assumptions that underpinned them, such as using evidence derived from:

> *information we gathered through Effective Early Learning, sustained shared thinking with the children, from feedback from parents around children and changes they had noticed in the children at home, through feedback from other members of staff. One of the most recent things we have just developed is [a. . .] 'listening to children' policy.*
>
> (Practice leader, case study 4)

Practice leaders who worked closely with staff in this way were able to work in greater depth with colleagues, spending time both modelling practice and using techniques such as encouraging experienced practitioners to promote and facilitate reflection on learning and the quality of interactions:

> *Part of what I have been doing through training and development work with staff is using different mechanisms to identify when learning's taking place [. . .] looking at the EYFS in more depth, using video more for reflection.*
>
> (Practice leader, LS29)

A common thread among these practice leaders was that they had the opportunity to develop a long-term vision for their settings focused on continuous improvement (see case study 4). Such notions led to the deployment of a wide range of tools to audit the quality of provision and monitor the changes they implemented:

> *The initiative was actioned by an audit carried out with the speech and language therapist, which enabled targets to be set for developing the language-friendly programme. The initial audit inspired the EYP to tackle the problem.*

(LS13 case report)

These practice leaders had integrated consideration of children's perspectives into their overall way of working with children to the extent that they were able to co-construct aspects of their learning environment and activities. They had built up a coherent programme to enable children to take ownership of their learning and to be involved in designing it throughout their time in the setting. These practice leaders valued developing children's ability to be critical and recognised that they needed to give them the confidence, opportunity and language to do this. This was part of an inclusive ethos that treated children's perspectives as both an important quality assurance process and a key outcome for children:

> *It's vital to improving provision and keeping provision at its best level because unless you are listening to children, you are missing out on a whole part of the picture. We could provide what we think is perfect equipment. We could provide what we think the parents would like to see but if it's not meeting the children's needs or what they want and we're not listening to them about that, that's a third of that equation out. In fact it's a much bigger part of the equation because it's the children's nursery.*

(Practice leader, case study 4)

In contrast, in the **established** settings, external frameworks, such as the EYFS, were used but were heavily mediated by practice leaders. They interpreted how key ideas would look in practice and underpinned them by drawing on wider theoretical understanding:

> *All staff use EYFS to do the planning [. . .] There is a lot of guidance through the EYFS that in itself sets a level of how to work, the areas you need to be covering. Then, we do lots of training for us and staff around small aspects of the EYFS and that feeds into the quality of understanding and how we implement it.*

(Practice leader, case study 1)

Practice leaders in these settings also faced external pressures to shape their view of quality provision to match others' expectations. Their confidence in their own professional theories of process quality helped them to mediate and, in some cases, resist such conflicting influences, as one practice leader whose nursery was part of an independent school explained: '*In a setting like this, it's about getting that balance in meeting the expectation of the school, the EYFS and the parent's expectations*' (Practice leader, LS61). To establish and legitimise her view of high quality pedagogy, this practice leader set out to introduce a pedagogical approach more closely based on early years practice into the school's reception class. Her success reduced the pressure on her to change her way of working. Thus, in practice, the ability of these practice leaders to establish a more expansive notion of quality depended on their ability both to develop norms in their settings and to deal effectively with external pressures to adopt more formal learning approaches.

Practice leaders in these settings tended to draw on children's perspectives as a form of consultation, through which they tried to solidify their views of current provision and how it could be improved. They focused their work on encouraging children to participate in the consultations and used a range of inclusive activities to develop children's ability to express their views, ensuring that they developed the language to do so:

> *The ethos runs throughout the nursery right from babies' room, so it's a gradual process but begins with listening to babies and is the same for the under threes as over threes.*
>
> (Practice leader, case study 1)

Finally, in the **emergent** settings there was rather less evidence of strategic assessments of quality based on a coherent overall vision of process quality. They tended to use instrumental measures of quality and outcomes for children drawn from external frameworks, for example, by assessing children's progress through observations based on the EYFS framework: '*We went through one area at each staff meeting and highlighted where we were and looked at what we could do to be better*' (Practice leader, LS11). There were relatively few examples of systematic assessment of the quality of practitioners' interactions with children or of the environment and pedagogical framing. None of these settings made regular use of a research-based tool such as ECERS or ITERS to assess the quality of provision. In addition, the link between assessments of children and developing the curriculum or pedagogical interactions on offer was limited or in the early stages of development and was often a focus of change during the period of research:

> *There is an evaluation that goes up on the wall every week of the children's learning. Although it's focused on the children and what*

> *they are learning, it actually reflects back on the key worker and the staff who have done that piece of work or were involved in that activity.*
>
> (Practice leader, LS20)

Overall, in these settings the focus on pedagogical framing appeared to be based on the need to get this in place before moving on to the more challenging area of interactions: '*At the moment [interaction] is not a priority but it is something I need to keep monitoring*' (Practice leader, LS01). Some of these settings had started from low bases in terms of practitioner–child interactions and had gone through lengthy change processes to influence them:

> *[Interaction] was flagged up first by Ofsted, which was four years ago, so that was something that we needed to improve on [. . .] Originally, it was getting the staff to be with the children at that level, moving around more and being aware of the children and where they were. And now the next bit, which has probably taken over a year, is to improve the quality of adults' interactions with the children, so we have got more quantity now, they are interacting more with the children, but now it is the quality issue of how they are interacting [that we are focusing on].*
>
> (Practice leader, LS20)

By the end of the study, many of these settings had begun to look at how to assess and improve the quality of their interactions with children, as case study 2 illustrates. In one setting, the practice leader had a strong vision for the setting she owned but this centred on developing further its caring ethos, which she saw as an essential precursor to learning: '*They would never learn anything if they didn't have the social and emotional things in place to start with*' (LS11). This appeared to have prevented her from focusing more extensively on pedagogical framing and interactions.

In these settings, if children's perspectives were considered they tended to be seen primarily in terms of expanding children's choices and access to resources and activities. Practice leaders were limited in their approaches to getting children to articulate their perspectives and lacked a repertoire of approaches and techniques. In many cases, the lack of a clearly articulated vision of process quality was also determined by contextual factors. For example, the process of developing a clear vision could be undermined by pressure to meet external improvement targets:

> *All of the areas I identified are linked to the centre's improvement plan and are also linked to my performance management targets.*

*The centre is also aware of the need to find ways to record and show
the impact that the centre has on the local community.*

(Practice leader, LS20)

Establishing a common understanding of the improvements that were required and developing norms around quality

The extent to which practice leaders had to drive improvement varied across
the settings. In some cases, specific interventions or projects were used to
engage staff, alongside formal CPD; in others, leaders used more informal
approaches, such as modelling, especially in relation to improving pedagogical interactions.

In the **emergent** settings, which were often working at relatively low
levels of process quality at the beginning of the research, communication
about what needed to be changed was often direct and challenging:

*I would start out by observing practice and pinpointing things that
are shouting out to me. Then [. . .] we would have a team meeting, I
would air my views and what I'm thinking about doing and why,
and get some feedback from the staff.*

(Practice leader, LS09)

As case study 1 illustrates, practice leaders appeared to see this as a
necessary stage in improving quality, which needed to be raised to a certain
level, before the understanding of staff was sufficient for them to be given
more autonomy:

*It was sort of quite directive to begin with, keeping it quite simple
and quite specific about things. Now we are trying to get it so that it
is less specific but more suggestive so that staff hopefully will then
take on the suggestions and develop it themselves.*

(Practice leader, LS20)

However, communicating what needed to be changed was not simply a
case of articulating the problems and ways forward. At a micro level, especially with staff who might not have witnessed high quality provision before,
practice leaders recognised the need to model the interactions and behaviours
they wanted to see, although a number struggled to find the time to do so: '*Her
absence from the nursery restricts opportunities to model practice and offer
support and guidance to staff in developing, implementing and reviewing
change*' (LS01 case report). This was also reflected in another setting, which
underlined the potential fragility of quality improvement in the emergent

settings. Here substantial improvements in elements of the framing pedago-gies between our second and third visits to the setting were initially reversed as a consequence of the practice leader leaving the setting before they had been systematically embedded into practice.

> *The interaction and developing relationships with children day-to-day needed to be addressed. But rather than that [being] something that just happened and then tailed off again, there needed to be some kind of system behind it that kept the momentum going and kept it building all the time.*
>
> (Practice leader, LS52)

However, the EYP continued to advise the setting and, by the end of the study, there was evidence that this 'dip' in process quality was being reversed.

In the **established** settings, practice leaders were less directive about what had to be improved: '*The way she works with staff is not to give them the answer but to explore with them the options*' (Manager, case study 1). They focused more on developing reflectivity and criticality among staff in relation to their own practice and provision more generally: '*The room leaders I wanted to be empowered and to be able to talk to staff, understanding what good practice was as opposed to "This is what we do here"* ' (EYP, case study 1). Developing such norms started with induction for new staff, who were gradually introduced to the setting's concept of quality provision. The growing emphasis in some of these settings on distributing practice leadership in their structures during the course of the research generated opportunities for more individualised feedback to spread responsibility for the improvement required:

> *I have meetings with the key workers every month to discuss any issues, problems or ideas that we were thinking about to take them forward, but they can come to me anytime. In the meetings we discuss other issues like planning, paperwork and ideas that they may want [to try] to help support the children.*
>
> (Practice leader, LS18)

There was also a move away from blanket observations of all children to more targeted detailed observations that enabled more in-depth under-standings of play and child development, as well as how their provision could influence this.

In many of the **embedded** settings, a culture had developed that prioritised the quality of interactions with children. From staff induction onwards, this norm was established and reinforced so that staff became used to certain ways of working. In one setting, in which even induction focused on pedagogical interactions, new members of staff were encouraged to learn from observing others: '*I have just picked up on what the other playworkers do and tried to fit in. It comes across in the planning meetings too*' (Practitioner, LS06).

These norms were reinforced through ongoing professional development and joint planning with practitioners but also informally via '*lots of chat and also, where we are able to [. . .] some timetabled opportunities away from the children to plan*' (Practice leader, case study 4). This was also sometimes formalised. In the same setting, one of the practice leaders tried to build coherence by instigating a review of the setting's policies that focused on the link between quality provision and positive outcomes for children:

> *We are reviewing our policies and this is something I have initiated, putting them all out for staff to discuss [. . .] We are also evolving children's wellbeing and their involvement levels, we're trying to bring all the bits together.*
>
> (Practice leader, case study 4)

Developing, leading and evaluating professional development activities that focused on improving process quality

As the preceding discussion has indicated, settings used a range of profes-sional activities to improve quality. These have been examined using three categories for analysing CPD (Kennedy, 2005):[5] transmission, transitional and transformative. Kennedy associates the move towards transformative approaches with increasing capacity for professional autonomy, which is analogous to the increasing capacity for practice leadership observed in some settings.

The **embedded** group of settings established a philosophy which reflec-ted Kennedy's (2005) characterisation of transformative professional develop-ment by integrating a range of approaches which highlighted their approach to child development: '*You've got to try and do it from different angles and different areas and it's basically looking at the ways people learn and trying to make sure you cover all the aspects – which is what we should be doing for children*' (Practice leader, LS08). Thus, the approaches used varied, depend-ing on the capacity available and what settings were trying to achieve. Their practice leaders often had roles that connected managing improvements with overall responsibility for quality assurance and staff development (see, for example, case studies 3 and 4). Indeed, one of the major advantages of having established practice leadership roles that encompassed these key areas of responsibility was being able to integrate improvement efforts with CPD so that they reinforced each other across the setting:

> *The EYP's strategy was to dovetail reforms that complement each other on to existing practices [. . .] The EYP initiates the reform, which she has 'picked up' from her practice networks and leverages external authority and internal expertise in order to validate the reform for staff. She then uses a part cascade training, part mentoring model based on the room system to embed the reform.*
>
> (LS13 case report)

Recognition of the need for sustained and differentiated staff development in order to embed change was another common element. Moreover, the strategic overview that some of these practice leaders had established also allowed them to move beyond providing CPD and enhance and refresh their colleagues' career development and practice by moving them between rooms and settings.

> *If you are doing the same job in the same setting for six years, you are going to get bored [. . .] So what I do is move staff around. They usually stay somewhere for two years and I move them on somewhere else. But I do try to look at who I'm putting them in with and what their strengths are and putting teams in that will have a roundedness.*
>
> (Practice leader, LS08)

The **established** settings had started to create their own distinct approaches to staff development. For example, in one setting professional development was designed to reflect and model the same values and pedagogical processes staff were being encouraged to use in their interactions with children:

> *We feel very strongly about treating staff the way we treat children. So it's about respect, positive reinforcement, so if someone does something really nice we would say, 'Wow! I loved the way you spoke to the children. I loved the way the children were interacting with you.'*
>
> (Practice leader, case study 1)

They tended to use relatively few transmission-based approaches to professional development and, where external training was used, they rejected the 'cascade' approach in favour of approaches like sending several staff members to the same session to build enthusiasm and momentum for change: *'Like the book area – you don't get the enthusiasm from your colleagues if you are just sharing your training with them. If they go on the training they will come back enthusiastic and keen to develop it'* (Practice leader, LS61).

The emphasis in these settings was on high involvement, transitional CPD approaches such as mentoring and coaching, buddying systems and peer observations, many of which combined to develop communities of practice. Such approaches encouraged greater professional autonomy and supported staff in exchanging knowledge and insights with each other. Practice leaders still led the activities but encouraged other staff to share their learning, particularly through modelling: *'Role modelling which is incredibly important [is] a huge way to show staff good interaction and we work really hard with that. The thoroughly experienced staff are encouraging the less experienced staff'* (Practice leader, case study 1).

Such approaches created a much wider range of learning relationships than could be facilitated by the lone practice leader. However, there were still relatively limited opportunities for staff to become involved in development and improvement processes, as the emphasis tended to remain on merely consulting staff on areas of concern.

Although in the **emergent** settings, there was a strong practical commitment to providing ongoing training and professional development for staff, there was widespread reliance on traditional, transmission-based CPD approaches. This often took the form of explicit training based on a deficit model,[6] designed to fill gaps in practitioners' knowledge: *'We sit down in our staff meetings and talk and I also do presentations'* (Practice leader, case study 2). A 'cascade' approach to sharing expertise was frequently used, with practice leaders generally sharing the knowledge and insights they had developed from CPD or from their engagement with professional networks. However, in some settings, practice leaders struggled to provide in-house CPD because of other commitments and were reliant on the availability of free external training and the goodwill of staff to invest in their own development:

> *If it was a course they wanted to do then that's fine; I can't always pay for it [. . .] if it were a course that needed to be paid for, then if it was in their own time at night, that's fine. If it was one that was through the day and you had to pay for it, then they would have to do that in their own time, like a day's holiday or something.*
>
> (Practice leader, LS11)

Practice leaders in these settings also addressed issues such as the development of sustained shared thinking and pedagogical framing issues such as the balance between child-initiated and adult-led activities. However, in contrast with the other groups of settings, they were much less likely to be the subject of sustained interventions or to use high-involvement development activities such as mentoring or observation and feedback.

Enhancing practice leadership capacity in the setting by connecting individuals and building teams

In many ways, the three outcomes already associated with practice leadership in action come together in the final outcome of enhancing practice leadership capacity in settings. Practice leaders drew on their strategic vision, shared understandings of the need for improvement and CPD approaches to develop supportive, shared cultures which allowed colleagues to enact practice leadership, building their sense of professional identity and agency to encourage them and their colleagues to take risks and ownership of change.

Although the majority of practice leaders in the **emergent** settings were senior managers, for many practice leadership was still a relatively undeveloped element of their role, which in turn limited their ability to develop practice leadership in others. The area in which gaining EYPS had had the biggest impact for them was in their approach to leadership. They had developed their understanding of the need to involve staff more widely in the process of change by being invitational and supportive of risk taking:

> *By allowing people to feel that they can contribute, although sometimes their contribution is not the thing that we want and by giving them a say, opportunities to discuss where the vision is coming from. If they come up with an idea, you will allow them to carry on with it.*
>
> (Practice leader, LS20)

The nature of the settings, particularly their size and practice leaders' role and position in them, was a key factor in limiting leaders' ability to develop or influence practice leadership at all levels from the macro to the micro. Thus, the manager of a small private nursery could influence practitioners' interactions with children because she was able to work hands on with them for up to four days a week and had a settled staff of seven (LS11). This was more challenging for a children's centre teacher working across two sites who was responsible for curriculum, planning and assessment *and* strategy (LS01). In another setting, in which the practice leader described her role as '*the link between management and practice*' (LS52), she also emphasised the importance of challenging staff norms and expectations through encouraging them to reflect and try new approaches:

> *It's really difficult because you don't want to sort of sit them down and say, 'I'm going to tell you how to talk to children'. That's when the modelling issue came up again because it's like, 'I'm doing this but are they actually paying any attention?' I feel that the staff I've got now are more receptive.*
>
> (Practice leader, LS52)

Overall, many EYPs in these settings had not established practice leadership beyond themselves and therefore found it difficult to work with the intensity required to bring about changes to all aspects of their settings' process quality. Leadership was less likely to be distributed or hybrid in these settings although, as case study 2 indicates, some practice leaders in these settings recognised this and had begun to connect colleagues to share responsibility for some areas of improvement.

There were more opportunities to distribute leadership responsibility in the **established** settings. Building additional practice leadership capacity was a developmental focus in these settings, whether it involved encouraging a relatively junior staff member to take on a leadership role:

> *[The manager] said to me, 'You can lead good practice within the setting. You don't have to have the official title.'*
> (Practice leader without formal leadership responsibility, LS61)

or completely re-configuring the senior leadership team to promote practice leadership:

> *After completing EYP I was asked to join the Leaders Learning Together network – a monthly meeting for nine months focusing on quality. As a result I have now identified senior leaders in each room. Because of the benefits of having [the EYP] in the bigger room, I think it is important that each room does have a leader.*
> (Manager, LS18)

Like case study 3, this reflects a movement towards Gronn's notion of leadership as 'configuration' in which multiple interdependent leadership elements facilitate a 'plurality of pathways to the achievement of successful organizational outcomes.'[7] After the manager in this setting also gained EYPS, she became more involved in practice in the setting and began explicitly to focus on team building to share more responsibility for planning and the curriculum with the existing EYP: '*My role as practice leader has helped me promote the importance of team work and sharing thoughts and ideas to achieve a shared goal [. . .] We now talk a lot about thoughts and ideas and what we plan to do next*' (Practice leader, LS18). In these settings, the acceptance of the need to develop practice leadership depended on the practice leader either occupying a senior leadership role or having their capacity to lead improvement recognised by a senior leader.

Finally, in the **embedded** settings, approaches were more flexible. Stretching practice leadership in and across settings took a number of forms, which came closer to realising Gronn's (2011) dynamic notion of hybridised leadership. In some settings this was achieved by developing a new leadership role between and alongside established formal positions (see case study 3), in others it was grafted on to existing structures, while in a third group it was consciously distinguished from routine management activity:

> *We have been here longer than the EYP role has existed so we built the role of the EYP around the areas that we needed. We've also tried to keep it separate from the management role. So the EYP is about day-to-day practice and management would be about managing people and instructions.*
>
> (Practice leader, case study 4)

This kind of approach was seen more often in some of the larger settings. In smaller settings where there was less room for manoeuvre, practice leadership was embedded less through defining new roles or changing structures and more through integrating it into the culture of the settings, which allowed them to 'grow their own' practice leaders: *'The previous EYP left but the new EYP was already here and inspired by the ethos of the setting. Even with a change in leader and two new members of staff in the last two months, things have stayed relatively consistent'* (Practitioner, LS06).

Summary

This chapter has introduced and exemplified the developmental model that we created out of our research to depict practice leadership in action. The model identifies four key outcomes associated with effective practice leadership and improvements to the quality of provision in the settings we researched, distinguishing settings according to three stages of practice leadership development. Chapter 5 exemplifies the model in more detail with four case studies of practice leadership from contrasting settings.

Notes

1   For an overview, see Robinson, V., Hohepa, M. and Lloyd, C. (2009) *School Leadership and Student Outcomes: Identifying What Works and Why: Best Evidence Synthesis Iteration [BES]*. Wellington, NZ: Ministry of Education; and for studies focusing on early childhood leadership in particular, see Heikka, J. and Hujala, E. (2013) Early childhood leadership through the lens of distributed leadership, *European Early Childhood Education Research Journal*, 21 (4), 568–80; Aubrey, C. (2011) *Leading and Managing in the Early Years*, 2nd edn. London: Sage; Aubrey, C., Godfrey, R. and Harris, A. (2013) How do they manage? An investigation of early childhood leadership, *Educational Management Administration and Leadership*, 41 (5), 5–29.

2   Siraj-Blatchford, I. and Manni, L. (2007) *Effective Leadership in the Early Years Sector*. London: Institute of Education, University of London; Hannah, S.

and Lester, P. (2009) A multilevel approach to building and leading learning organizations, *The Leadership Quarterly*, 20, 34–48.

3   Siraj-Blatchford and Manni (2007).

4   Gronn, P. (2011) Hybrid configurations of leadership, in A. Bryman, D. Collinson, K. Grint, B. Jackson and M. Uhl-Bien (eds.) *Sage Handbook of Leadership*. London: Sage.

5   Kennedy, A. (2005) Models of continuing professional development: a framework for analysis, *Journal of In-Service Education*, 31 (2), 235–50.

6   Ibid.

7   Gronn (2011), at p. 447.

5 Four practice leadership case studies

This chapter is made up of detailed case studies of practice leadership in four settings, which, taken together, represent a range of structures, contexts and approaches to developing practice leadership and early years provision. The case studies draw on interviews with practitioners and observations of practice, as well as analysis of the settings' shifting formal and informal leadership structures, in order to examine evidence of their improvement over time. They are intended to illustrate in detail many of the themes, issues and challenges relating to practice leadership outlined in Chapters 1–4.

Case study 1 is a voluntary setting in North London with 60 children on roll. Having introduced a flat leadership structure, the setting was attempting to empower room leaders to lead improvement. Case study 2 is a small community nursery, also in North London, with 17 children aged over three on roll. It was focusing on changes to curriculum planning and the learning environment as means of rapidly improving provision. Case study 3 depicts a group of three private nurseries in the East Midlands, with a total of around 140 children on roll, which was using a national speech/language and communication initiative as a lever for change. Finally, case study 4 explores practice leadership in a private setting serving the community around a university in the South East. It also had around 60 children from a range of backgrounds on roll. The setting's priority for change was improving the quality, and quality assurance, of provision.

Taken as a group, the case studies illustrate different aspects of practice leadership, all of which were viable approaches developed in response to the context in which practitioners worked. The case studies also reveal settings at different stages of a continuum of quality improvement, from a rapidly improving setting looking to embed positive change throughout (case study 2) to a setting that maintained high quality provision over an extended period (case study 4). The names of settings and individuals have been changed throughout.

Case study 1: Building practice leadership capacity at multiple levels in a large setting

The setting

Case study 1 (LS49) depicts a voluntary setting in a large five-storey Victorian house in an affluent part of North London. It had around 60 children on roll and around 24 members of staff. The children were separated by age on different floors of the building and only a small number had learning difficulties or spoke English as an additional language. Nena was the only EYP in the setting at the beginning of the study, although two of her colleagues, the family liaison officer and one of the room leaders, also gained EYPS during the research. She had over 20 years' experience of working with children under five and was one of the two 'lead practitioners' in the setting.

Formal leadership structure

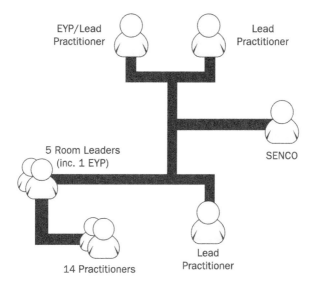

Figure 5.1   Formal leadership structure.

Being, becoming and developing as a practice leader

Nena became one of two lead practitioners in the setting, along with the setting's manager, when she gained EYPS through the Short pathway in 2007, although another lead practitioner was appointed subsequently as Figure 5.1 illustrates. This signalled an explicit move away from occupying a 'management' role towards working on a more equal basis with practitioners, as the other lead practitioner explained:

> *We work closely together, we are both lead practitioners, we do lots of training together, we support each other on a daily basis. I would describe my leadership and [Nena's] leadership as equal.*

Nena's primary focus was on leading practice in the setting, whereas her fellow lead practitioner oversaw families joining the nursery. To do this, Nena led training and mentored colleagues at a meso level, as well as working directly with children and maintaining and updating policies at a macro level (see Chapter 3 for a discussion of these leadership levels). She felt that she developed significantly after she gained EYPS, which made her better equipped both to identify the need for improvement and to implement change: '*[EYPS] gave me that professional confidence to go forward with what we wanted to do as a setting*'. She also felt that EYPS increased her repertoire of strategies for leading practice, which '*made a huge difference to being able to support colleagues*'.

Practice leadership

Nena and her fellow lead practitioner shared the leadership of the setting in an increasingly flat structure, an approach they attempted to extend throughout the setting as the research progressed. For example, they worked hard to develop macro strategies to ensure that staff and all those involved in the setting had a shared and clear expectation of the type of provision they were trying to develop and the values that underpinned it, as Nena emphasised:

> *We do a lot with vision [. . .] We invite staff to come along and hear what we say to parents so that they know what our practice is about, which is one tiny way of doing that. We have staff who have been here for a long time and they are fully on board and they believe that in the same way we do with passion.*

As already indicated, they also placed a strong emphasis on professional development, mixing internal provision with external training and using a range of high involvement professional development processes which functioned at both meso and micro levels, as Nena explained:

> *Mentoring and coaching is a huge part of what I do now, leading practice and having a really good knowledge of the EYFS, encouraging staff to use it as much as possible on a day-to-day basis and to help [them] with their planning and evaluation and stuff [. . .] We need to give new staff lots of good role modelling, lots of workshops to get them hopefully to see the values that we have.*

Their emphasis on supporting new staff and improving staff retention also resulted in the introduction of a buddy system. This system was initiated by Nena and
focused on ensuring that Level 3 practitioners could access support and advice
from an experienced practitioner who was outside the management team.

Developing practice leadership capacity

As outlined towards the end of Chapter 3, we used social network analysis
(SNA) to examine the shifts in professional networks in the setting during the
research. The sociograms in Figures 5.2 and 5.3 indicate the responses when
staff were asked to identify up to three people in the setting to whom they had
gone for advice and support about developing children's learning in the
preceding 12 months. The individuals with most lines attached to them were
the most commonly cited sources of guidance. When they were first asked this
question in the first iteration of the survey (Figure 5.2), the overwhelming
proportion of staff who responded indicated that they went to either Nena or
the other lead practitioner (or both), reflecting the ongoing influence of the
setting's previous, more hierarchical structure.

As Figure 5.3 reveals, when the same question was asked a year later,
following the work on empowering room leaders, responses were much more
evenly distributed among staff in the setting, resulting in a much more

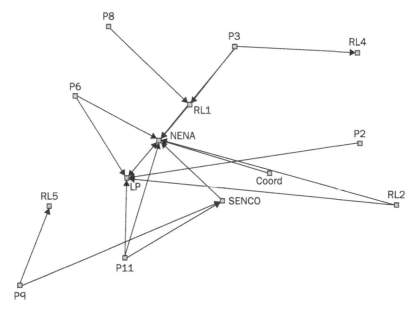

Figure 5.2 Sources of advice or support about developing children's learning (SNA
survey 1).

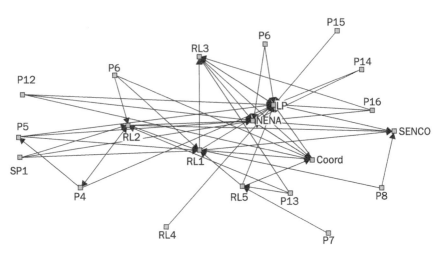

Figure 5.3   Sources of advice or support about developing children's learning (SNA survey 2).

complex sociogram. Two of the room leaders (RL1 and RL2) and the setting's coordinator had become much more central sources of advice and support for their colleagues by this point.

As the discussion at the end of Chapter 3 indicates, this pattern of growing decentralization and increasingly dense interrelationships persisted to the end of the research (see Figures 3.14 and 3.15 in Chapter 3), with a series of mini-networks developing to provide nested support across a range of areas.

Improving the quality of provision

The setting's focus during the research on the empowerment of room leaders was both a response to the structural barrier of high staff turnover and part of an explicit strategy to encourage staff to take on more responsibility for improving the quality of provision. In Nena's words, *'it's about staff reflecting on what their roles are about'* and about them attempting to develop a more consistent approach to practice and practice leadership throughout the setting. To support the emergent practice leadership of the room leaders at the meso level, Nena developed a series of leadership workshops for them that she ran in-house but which were informed by leadership training she and the other lead practitioner had attended. As she said, the workshops emphasised the importance of reflecting and working on existing problems: *'[We] felt it is important that room leaders feel confident within their rooms and are able to lead the room, rather than manage it, and get everyone on board.'*

The work with room leaders created a network of learning relationships that connected staff across the setting. The SNA data illustrated in Figures 5.2

and 5.3 shows the central position of several staff members in supportive networks, giving advice to other staff. These networks overlapped with the formal leadership structures and revealed the extent to which Nena's colleagues had accepted her practice leadership role. This had changed whom staff sought out for support and was underlined by the fact that, by the end of the study, most room leaders tended to discuss practice in their room or with other room leaders before they went to the manager or Nena:

> *Initially, new staff would come to me or [the other lead practitioner] but now they don't come as much. Now they go to any of the room leaders for advice. [. . .] It's not about what we do here, it's the guidelines of the EYFS, everything is a backup. We do what we are doing here because it's the right thing to practise. I wanted room leaders not just to understand that but also relate that to others.*

This had not only deepened the kinds of conversations Nena was having with staff, it had also improved the consistency and speed with which practice issues were dealt with and new ideas taken up in the nursery:

> *Because the room leaders were feeling empowered, they were facilitating staff to be empowered within the room. So anything that these new staff were learning from the workshops was coming through to the children much quicker than it would do if we didn't have these workshops.*

At the same time, improvements were found in the overall quality of provision in the setting. In terms of the observations undertaken in the study in relation to process quality, case study 1 improved the most dramatically of all the settings. Its baseline score for pedagogical framing (using ECERS-R) increased from below the mean for all the settings to above average, and it was one of the three settings in the study to show educationally significant improvements in terms of both framing pedagogies and the quality of pedagogical interactions (PCIT). In relation to pedagogical interaction, it also showed the highest improvement score of all the settings, moving from being below average to clear indications of significant improvement in all areas (see Figure 5.4).

Large increases were also observed in key elements of the ECERS-E observations (mathematics, literacy), which have been associated with positive outcomes for children's development, with the scores increasing significantly to the maximum possible for each of the items illustrated in Figure 5.5.

During the observation period, Nena felt that *'we've made constant improvements through self-reflection, self-evaluation'* and that this had become part of the culture of the setting. It was also clear to her that the fact that two further staff members gained EYPS after the formal conclusion of

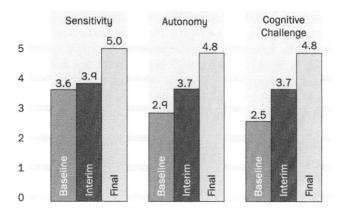

Figure 5.4 PCIT scores for sensitivity, autonomy and cognitive challenge averaged for baseline, interim and final observations.

the research was a positive outcome that would help embed improvements and distribute practice leadership further in the setting.

This case study has illustrated the ways in which the setting introduced a flatter structure in which responsibility for leading practice was distributed throughout a large setting, leading to improvement in the overall quality of provision. The second case study focuses on how a single practice leader in a much smaller setting began to share practice leadership in a conscious attempt to deepen its positive impact on the quality of provision.

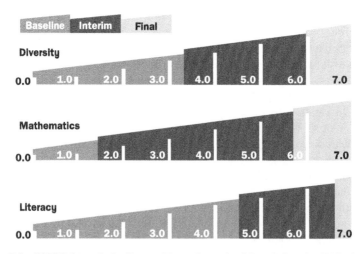

Figure 5.5 ECERS-E trends for literacy (L), mathematics (M) and diversity (D) for baseline, interim and final observations.

Case study 2: Deepening the impact of practice leadership in a small setting

The setting

Case study 2 (LS22) focuses on a small, voluntary setting for children aged over three located on the lower floor of a community centre in a deprived part of North London. Revitalised from 2009 when Clara, its only EYP, joined the setting as manager, during the research it had around 17 children on roll, mainly boys aged over three of Afro-Caribbean descent. The majority of the children spent 10 hours a day in the setting, which had a major refurbishment during the study. The fairly stable staff team had eight members, mostly from black or minority ethnic backgrounds including Clara herself (see Figure 5.6). She was the only EYP in the setting and had worked with children under five for over 21 years. Clara's overall objective during the research period was to expand the setting and deepen the impact of the positive changes already introduced, which she did during the research period by focusing on enhancing curriculum planning and the learning environment. As a result, the setting, which was below average in terms of quality scores at the beginning of the study, had improved significantly by the end of the research.

Formal leadership structure

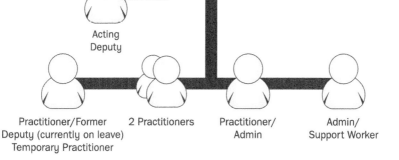

Figure 5.6 Formal leadership structure.

Being, becoming and developing as a practice leader

Clara gained EYPS in 2007 via the Validation pathway. She was highly experienced and was appointed as manager in 2009, explicitly because she had EYPS, in order to expand the setting and improve its practice and provision. Clara described the status as *'the backbone of what I have become'* because it had validated her knowledge and experience and supported her in the changes she had made in the setting. Her development during the research focused on moving from introducing 'quick wins' into the setting, notably by enhancing the learning environment, to beginning to embed deeper improvement by starting to distribute the responsibility for change, especially in relation to the quality of planning and pedagogical interactions.

Practice leadership

In many ways, by the end of the research case study 2 was in a similar position to that which case study 1's setting occupied at the beginning of the research period. During the first visits, Clara was clearly the sole practice leader. Her approach to leading practice was still fairly directive at the macro level at this point, reflecting the fact that she had been explicitly recruited to improve provision rapidly:

> *I am the core of the setting. That is why they employed me because I have an EYP status. It's hard, very hard, but [. . .] we are now a united team and we work together for the good of the setting.*

Her confidence was founded on her understanding of good practice: *'When [staff] realise that the way they are doing it is outdated and it isn't working effectively, then they will switch over to what [I am doing].'* At the same time, the small size of the setting allowed her to lead at the meso level, using a combination of in-house and external CPD:

> *We had a staff meeting and I talked about the development of the environment and I did a whole PowerPoint presentation to the staff [and] helped them to do some little exercises and activities within that [. . .] Also, I send my staff on various courses to implement and to ensure that the curriculum plan is stable and is firmly embedded in the whole nursery for the children's welfare.*

As well as improving key procedural elements of the setting such as planning and the learning environment, Clara modelled a commitment to improvement and learning which appeared to have had a positive effect on both children and staff in the setting. For example, she began a Masters in Educational Leadership and Management during the course of the research, partly in order to raise the aspirations of her colleagues through her emphasis on constantly improving and renewing her skills: *'Because they can see that I am pushing for more education [for myself], they are encouraged to do so as well. I am not just pushing them, I am pushing myself too.'*

Initially, Clara also operated at a micro level, modelling good practice to colleagues, again using the setting's small size to her advantage. However, as the improvements to the learning environment – and the planning processes in particular – began to have an impact, she was able to delegate more responsibility for areas such as behaviour management and ICT to her colleagues and concentrate more on strategic leadership. This is illustrated by the social network analysis undertaken during the research.

Developing practice leadership capacity

Figures 5.7 and 5.8 indicate the responses when staff were asked to identify up to three people on whom they relied for reassurance and support about work-related issues. The responses illustrated in Figure 5.7 underline the fact that this was a close-knit, small setting, with most practitioners naming Clara as the main source of support in the first iteration of the survey, reflecting her position as single practice leader at this point.

This broadly remained the case when the survey was repeated a year later, during which period Clara had begun to distribute responsibility more extensively among the staff. However, a small shift can be detected in Figure 5.8, indicating the increased centrality of other staff members in the network,

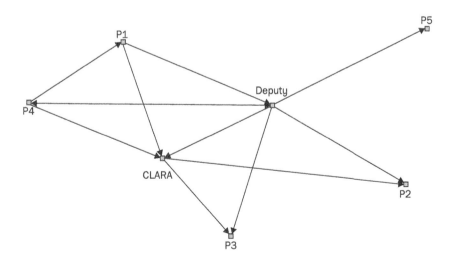

Figure 5.7 Sources of reassurance and support about work-related issues (SNA survey 1).

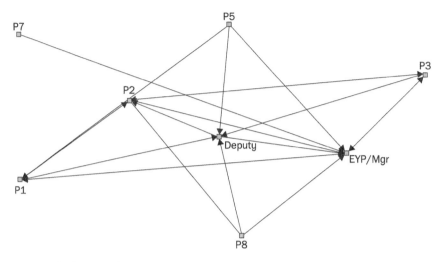

Figure 5.8 Sources of reassurance and support about work-related issues (SNA survey 2).

notably the setting's deputy and practitioner (P2). This pattern was repeated across the survey, with the exception of the setting's improvement strategy, where staff remained much more likely to rely on Clara.

Improving the quality of provision

During the study, the setting focused in particular on improving curriculum planning, working with an advisory teacher on *'evaluation, observation, planning and the paperwork that goes with it and how we can link everything together, including the environment, to enable children to have access to all the toys'*. Alongside a commitment to making learning 'fun', this was supported by a systematic approach to monitoring improvement, particularly in staff interactions with children. Initially, this was tightly scrutinized to effect change quickly, as Clara explained:

> *It's very rigid because I want to make sure that children are being interacted with and monitored regularly. Any issues lacking in practice will come up in meetings and [we will] discuss them and make sure that staff carry on interacting with children.*

This was not so much because of the cultural barrier of staff being reluctant to change their practice (see the discussion of barriers to improvement in Chapter 3). The issue was rather that staff had not always been exposed to new ideas or ways of working, and it took time for them to absorb the need for change and introduce new approaches into their work. Therefore, Clara was also careful to give her colleagues space to recognise what they wanted to improve, to take risks and to develop in their practice:

> *I allow them to make mistakes [. . .] As I watch things, they may come to me and say, 'So and so isn't working that way', so I say, 'Have you done this? Have you done that?' 'No, we have been doing what we were doing before.' So I say, 'Exactly, this is why it doesn't work and I have to allow you to see that it doesn't work in order for you to understand what I am giving you, the way I am pushing you forward.'*

As already indicated, she combined this kind of micro level support with access to external CPD to reduce their reliance on her for ideas. She also improved pedagogical framing by encouraging staff to rework curriculum planning to follow children's interests more effectively, using the EYFS to increase child-initiated activities:

> *Each child has a focus each week. The activities are set around the children's interest so there is an indirect impact on children as a result of making staff more focused on children's interests. [The staff] prefer it this way. They said to me, 'I am not going back to the old one, this one is easy, you can see what we are doing and we can see what everyone else is doing.'*

Towards the end of the research, staff were being encouraged to take more responsibility for improvement and, although this remained at a relatively early stage of development, changes such as the recruitment of a new deputy after the research formally concluded were indications that practice leadership was beginning to be shared more widely in an attempt to deepen the impact of change.

At the beginning of the study, the setting was rated satisfactory by Ofsted. By the end, it was rated outstanding. This judgement was supported by the fact that the setting showed some of the most significant increases in observed process quality, from one of the lowest starting points. Thus, the assessment of the quality of pedagogical framing (using ITERS-R) initially produced the second lowest average score for the learning environment but was just below the mean for all settings by the end of the study, having shown the greatest improvement of any settings in this respect. There was particular progress in listening and talking, one of the sub-scales associated in previous research with positive impacts on children's outcomes (see Figure 5.9).

The setting was also one of only three settings to have demonstrated educationally significant improvement in both pedagogical framing and pedagogical interactions with children. As Figure 5.10 indicates, outcomes

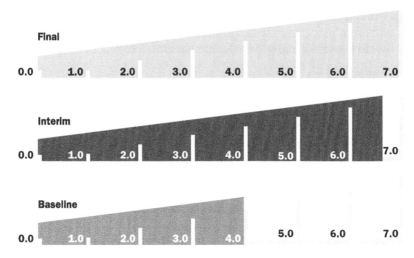

Figure 5.9 Changes in listening and talking sub-scales on ITERS-R observations.

from PCIT observations also improved significantly, again from a low base, in the areas of sensitivity and cognitive challenge, although they showed no increase in autonomy. However, the gap between Clara's scores and those of the practitioners widened during the study: she outscored practitioners by 1 point in each of the three areas during the final observations at the end of the research. This gap was even greater in terms of promoting sustained shared thinking, reflecting Clara's recognition that there was still progress to be made in embedding improved practice in the setting as a whole.

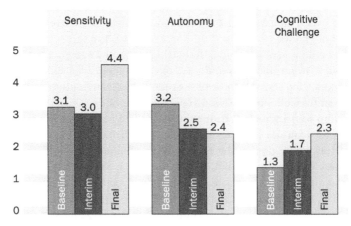

Figure 5.10 PCIT scores for sensitivity, autonomy and cognitive challenge averaged for baseline, interim and final observations.

This case study has focused on the challenges involved in beginning to distribute responsibility for practice leadership, following a period of rapid improvement, in order to sustain and deepen that change. Case study 3 is a pertinent contrast in that it examines the challenges faced by a practice leader in improving provision across a group of three settings.

Case Study 3: Improving quality through practice leadership across a group of settings

The setting

The setting in case study 3 (LS28) was made up of three private nurseries with a total of about 38 staff. It was located in a city in the East Midlands offering provision for children aged 0–5. Initially above average in terms of overall quality, the setting maintained this position during the study. Jill was the only EYP in the group throughout the period of research, working across the group as quality coordinator (see Figure 5.11). Her role was supernumerary and practice-oriented and she spent up to four days a week working directly with children, as well as leading new initiatives across the nurseries. She had over 20 years' experience of working with children under 5.

Formal leadership structure

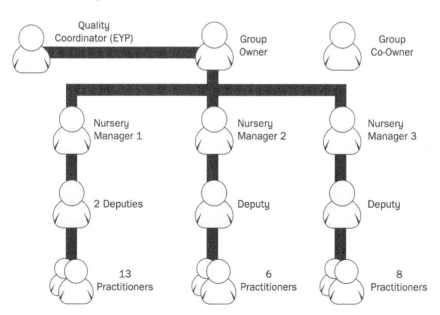

Figure 5.11 Formal leadership structure.

Being, becoming and developing as a practice leader

As quality coordinator, Jill was responsible for leading practice and quality assurance across the three nurseries in the group. She worked closely with practitioners and oversaw agreed areas of practice and policy:

> *I am the steer person in terms of the managers at the three nurseries in terms of pushing policies through. That's part of my job basically. It is given high priority at every management meeting throughout the year, it's my decision and I take away that feedback and put it into a new policy.*

Jill gained EYPS through the Short pathway in 2009, regarding it as a way to develop her career without having to move into formal management:

> *I just think there was nowhere else for us to go. You've got Level 3, you've got years and years of experience. If you don't want to be a teacher or run a children's centre and learn about multi-agency management and all of that, what else do you do?*

Although Jill did not feel that gaining the status offered her much that was new, *'for me the EYPS was really like the icing on the cake'*; its value for her was as a Level 6 qualification that validated her prior knowledge and experience:

> *I can make decisions now based on theories and a good knowledge of child development, which you learn through your degree and your Foundation Degree. Whereas your EYP gives you the name I suppose.*

Practice leadership

Jill's role as quality coordinator was practice focused and she spent up to four days in a typical week working directly with children. At the end of the study her time was fairly evenly split between children aged under two and those aged three to four years, but this depended on the needs of each nursery, agreed in conjunction with each manager. Her remaining time was spent leading, coordinating and evaluating practice and developing and delivering CPD. Her supernumerary role allowed her to meet the needs of the nurseries in the group at different levels of practice leadership. At a macro level, she held a strategic leadership role across the three settings, working closely with the three nursery managers to respond to their change aspirations and bringing in ideas and national initiatives such as Every Child a Talker (ECAT) from outside to improve practice. This required and enabled her to consider how the demands of competing and sometimes contradictory notions of quality needed to be balanced, integrated and sequenced across the three settings at a macro level.

Jill worked with all staff in the nurseries, particularly with room leaders and practitioners. In designing and delivering CPD, she therefore also worked at a meso level with groups and teams, working to embed improvements in practice. She also worked at a micro level with both room leaders and practitioners. With room leaders, Jill focused on developing their leadership to take on more responsibility for improving children's learning in the room:

> She [a room leader] does lack a lot of confidence, so change for [her] is perhaps a bigger thing than it would be for someone else [. . .] It's just finding little ways where they can't fail, nothing's going to be a disaster, but making sure you just help enough to nudge her and then you're there.

They were then encouraged to instil these ideas into their colleagues' practice in their rooms. Jill also worked at a micro level with practitioners, to whom she offered highly focused support for improvement and modelled what she expected them to do. These opportunities also allowed her to demonstrate to room leaders how they could lead practice. The key to this was Jill's supernumerary role, the influence of which is traced in the next section of the case study, and her close working relationship with the group's main co-owner. This allowed her to move staff (including herself) around to fill gaps or extend practice at micro and meso levels, particularly when a number of staff went on maternity leave.

Developing practice leadership capacity

The sociograms in Figures 5.12 and 5.13 indicate responses when staff were asked to name up to three people to whom they went for new ideas about improving practice in the settings. For case study 3, the sociograms included two or three of the settings in the group, depending on where Jill had been working most during the preceding period. Figure 5.12 illustrates responses to the second iteration of the SNA survey. In the months before this, Jill had been working intensively at Dove Hill (D) and the responses indicate that all the practitioners in that setting relied on both Jill and the recently appointed manager for new ideas. Although some practitioners at Westgrove (W), the largest setting in the group, also relied on Jill for new ideas, more went to their manager, reflecting the fact that Jill was spending the majority of her time at Dove Hill. However, beyond Jill there was relatively little collaboration between staff at the two settings at that time. The closed nature of the two

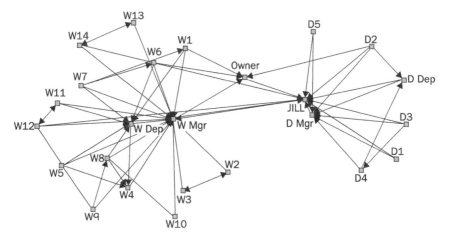

Figure 5.12 Sources of new ideas about improving practice in two settings (SNA survey 2).

settings, between which she was the main connective hub alongside the manager of the largest setting in the group, indicates the importance of her cross-setting, brokerage role.

Figure 5.13 indicates the responses from all three nurseries in the group after the third iteration at the end of the research. At Westgrove, most practitioners

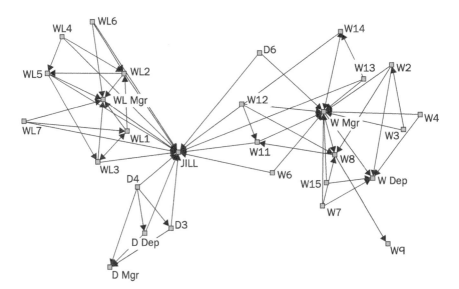

Figure 5.13 Sources of new ideas about improving practice in two settings (SNA survey 3).

still preferred to approach their manager for new ideas. However, all the practitioners who responded from Dove Hill and Windlowe (WL), the third setting in the group, named Jill, further emphasising the value and reach of her supernumerary role and her influence in all three nurseries. Figure 5.13 clearly illustrates Jill's uniquely central position across the group as a whole, indicating her work at macro, meso and micro levels. However, the three nurseries in the group remain almost entirely distinct, with the exception of practitioner D6 who had better links with Westgrove nursery.

This pattern was also reflected in the responses to the other areas explored in the survey, underlining both Jill's centrality in the group and the possible risks of relying on an individual to transfer practice and monitor quality and improvement across the group. The relatively limited evidence of professional relationships between staff in different nurseries may be inevitable given the relatively high levels of staff turnover during the research. However, there were indications of significant improvements in the quality of provision in each nursery in the group and early evidence of nurseries beginning to learn from each other.

Improving the quality of provision

The major priority for improving the quality of provision during the research was improving speech/language and communication through the introduction of ECAT. Gaining accreditation at Westgrove, the largest nursery in the group, was the culmination of 18 months' work, led by Jill working closely with one of the local authority's Early Language Consultants. In addition to building the portfolio of practice, the major challenge had been the structural issue of losing seven members of staff to maternity leave during the accreditation period. This made it difficult to maintain momentum post-accreditation and ensure that high standards in speech and language practice were sustained. ECAT was useful because it allowed Jill to focus on continuing to promote the use of the successful processes that had been introduced:

> *ECAT was the springboard for everything; it really was, everything. I can categorically tell you that all the changes we have made all came as a result of ECAT because it focuses on the language and communication and that's paramount, but it also teaches about how your environment can have an impact.*

Later in the study the focus shifted to transferring what they had learned to the other nurseries in the group, where Jill also used ECAT as a means of achieving wider improvements. This included encouraging staff from Westgrove to begin to work with their colleagues at Dove Hill:

> *The interactions, the planning, the activities, the environment, all of that has springboarded from [ECAT]. We try to raise everybody's practice in interaction and really think about how they can interact best with those children on that date in that activity, but also to make it more consistent throughout the nursery.*

Jill also used the ECAT framework to challenge accepted practice and encourage practitioners to consider children's learning and development more deeply:

> *Things like the nursery routine, encouraging the staff members to think, 'OK, that might suit that group of children on that day' [. . . have] opened up a lot more opportunities for the children for them to carry on and develop their thinking and what they want to do, knowing that the staff will support them and scaffold them and follow them.*

During the study, Westgrove was inspected by Ofsted and moved from being rated good to outstanding. Focusing on the two nurseries in which observation data were collected during the study, which were the core of Jill's improvement work during the period of the research, ratings of the pedagogical environment (using ITERS-R) were maintained at high levels overall in both settings and scores for pedagogical interactions (measured using PCIT) showed a significant increase in the area of sensitivity over the course of the research. Although this was not replicated in the areas of autonomy or cognitive challenge, instances of practitioners without EYPS engaging children in sustained shared thinking also increased. The high scores for practitioners at both Dove Hill (setting 2) and Westgrove (setting 1) in Figure 5.14 suggest that

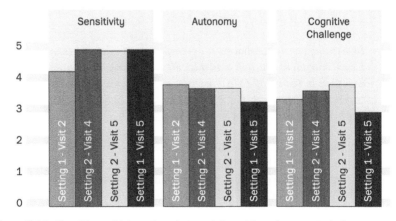

Figure 5.14 Practitioners' interactions in two of the settings in case study 3.

key elements of interactional process quality were increasingly embedded in both settings during the research, led by Jill as quality coordinator.

The key practice leadership challenge for Jill related to the difficulty of improving the quality of provision with a large staff group across three settings. The final case study focuses on a high quality setting that was successful in maintaining that quality over the course of the research.

Case Study 4: Establishing a common understanding of quality through practice leadership in a highly successful setting

Background

Case study 4 (LS19) describes a private nursery, attached to a university in South East England, with around 11 staff members (see Figure 5.15). During the research period it had two EYPs and the case study focuses on Carl, the only male EYP in the study, who was responsible for quality assurance and equality policy across the setting. Focusing on practice, he typically spent up to four days a week working directly with children aged 2–5. During the study, the setting's improvement strategy centred on implementing changes associated with the Effective Early Learning (EEL) project. Above average in terms of baseline quality at the beginning of the research, the setting improved further during the study.

Formal leadership structure

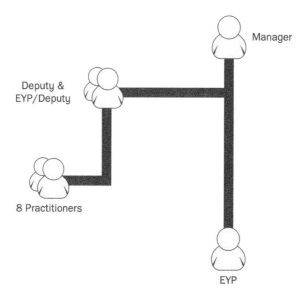

Figure 5.15   Formal leadership structure.

Being, becoming and developing as a practice leader

Highly experienced with over 20 years' experience of working with children aged under five, Carl gained EYPS via the Validation pathway in 2007. Although he did not have formal management responsibility, he oversaw quality assurance and equality policy in the nursery, working closely with its formal management team. One of the setting's two deputy managers, with whom Carl worked closely and who gained EYPS at the same time as him, was on maternity leave for the latter part of the research.

Carl's main motivation in gaining the status was to formalise and validate his experience and practice, as well as to give himself an opportunity to build on his experience without having to become a manager, echoing case study 3. It also improved his sense of professional status: *'The EYP affirmed what I do. My practice has to be good because of being very visible [as a male EYP], so it professionalised my role.'* Having responsibility for implementing the EEL programme also increased his experience of, and confidence in, leading colleagues. In addition, Carl felt that his and his colleagues' professional relationship was consolidated and enhanced by their having undertaken the status together. He felt this had *'had a positive influence in allowing us to review what we do as a nursery'*.

Practice leadership

Carl saw his role in leading practice as combining aspects of formal and informal leadership at different levels in the nursery. Although he was not formally part of the management team, he worked with the senior managers to improve the quality of provision at the macro level. His work with colleagues centred on supporting and mentoring them and modelling practice. He said that his conscious choice to inhabit an intermediary position between practitioners and the setting's management structure gave him space to influence colleagues in this way at both meso and micro levels: *'The fact that I'm not management allows me to have an input and sometimes conversations with members of staff that I wouldn't be able to otherwise.'* Central to this was being able to work in partnership with his fellow practice leader:

> We complement each other and complement each other's strengths. We support each other in developing other areas. We have been here longer than the EYP role has existed, so we built the role of the EYP around the areas that we needed. We've also tried to keep it separate from the management role, so the EYP is about day-to-day practice and the manager would be about managing people and instructions.

Developing practice leadership capacity

The social network analysis that was used to trace the flow of the setting's professional networks during the study illustrated some interesting shifts. When staff were first asked a series of questions about who they would go to for advice and support, no one was cited more than the setting's manager in any of the areas examined. When the survey was repeated a year later, Carl and the two deputy managers were also revealed as network hubs in most areas, with Carl most frequently cited in relation to new ideas about improving practice, advice about developing children's learning and, in particular, the EEL improvement focus, as Figure 5.16 illustrates.

This increasingly flat structure was even more apparent in the final survey at the end of the research. By this time Carl's quality assurance role was more embedded and he was regarded as the most common source of advice and support in all of the seven areas examined except, interestingly, new ideas about improving practice. This suggests that Carl's practice leadership influence increased as the study progressed and that his intermediary position leading practice between managers and practitioners appeared to be highly valued by his colleagues. By this time, all of the staff members who responded said they went to him for advice about the EEL improvement focus, as Figure 5.17 indicates.

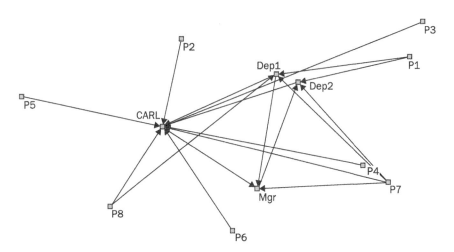

Figure 5.16 Sources of advice and support about the EEL project (SNA survey 2).

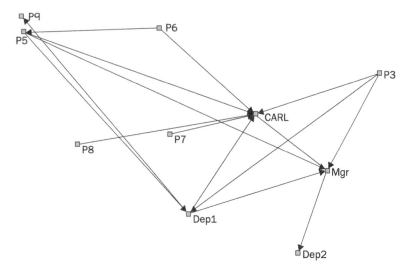

Figure 5.17 Sources of advice and support about the EEL project (SNA survey 3).

Improving the quality of provision

Carl's sustained work over three years on EEL was the major improvement focus in the setting during the course of the research. Impacts from the process included developing a 'listening to children' policy and integrating it into the setting's ethos and practice, as Carl outlined:

> It's vital to improving provision and keeping provision at its best level because unless you are listening to children, you are missing out on a whole part of the picture. We could provide what we think is perfect equipment. We could provide what we think the parents would like to see, but if it's not meeting the children's needs or what they want and we're not listening to them about that, that's a third of that equation out. In fact, it's a much bigger part of the equation because it's the children's nursery.

Effective Early Learning was implemented and evaluated through a combination of discussion and modelling practice with staff and feedback from parents. Carl also used it to refine existing processes, such as the setting's observation procedures, in order to improve practice and embed new practices and processes. This reflected his responsibility for quality and equality and the setting's inclusive ethos:

> [EEL] is embedded in what we do. Three years ago what we really needed to change what we were doing was the peer observation of other members of staff and overcoming what previously was not

quite fair, where people were worried about passing judgment or being judged and talking through those issues.

Thus, the major barrier to further improvement was cultural, although it was based on fear of failure rather than reluctance to change. Carl and his colleagues looked to sustain impact by working at different levels in the nursery to inculcate and embed a culture of taking risks. This helped ensure that staff had a shared understanding of why an improvement was necessary and how to achieve it, encouraging them to take on aspects of practice leadership. The setting's manager gave him time and support to do this and he drew on external support when necessary. This should be seen in the context of the setting's philosophy of continuous improvement, as Carl highlighted: *'There is always vision for more. There is always a very hugely positive vision to put forward.'* This philosophy was supported by the deployment of a wide range of tools and processes to audit the quality of provision and monitor the changes implemented in the setting.

Observations undertaken during the study suggested that the setting's emphasis on continuous improvement was having significant impact. Case study 4 was one of the settings that maintained high levels of quality in terms of both pedagogical framing and pedagogical interactions throughout the research. In terms of pedagogical framing, its baseline scores on ECERS-R and ECERS-E were above average throughout the study and improved in key areas such as activities, programme structure, literacy and diversity by the final observations.

In terms of pedagogical interactions, averaged overall scores increased in the areas of sensitivity, autonomy and cognitive challenge between baseline and final observations, as Figure 5.18 indicates, although the autonomy score

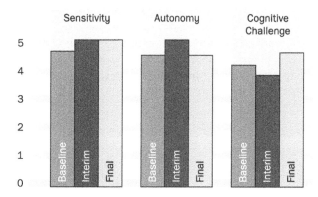

Figure 5.18 PCIT scores for sensitivity, autonomy and cognitive challenge averaged for baseline, interim and final observations.

fell back a little from the interim observation. In addition, the gap between averaged scores for Carl and practitioners without EYPS also closed in all three areas between the baseline and final visits, with the greatest reduction occurring in autonomy. This suggests that Carl's emphasis on modelling, along with improvements associated with EEL, had a positive impact on what was already a very effective setting at the beginning of the research.

Summary

The case studies in this chapter illustrate in detail how practice leaders worked to improve the quality of provision in a range of settings and contexts. They were all established practitioners before they gained EYPS, all having over 20 years' experience of working with children under five by the end of the research, but all took on new roles and responsibilities after gaining the status, which focused in different ways on using practice leadership to enhance the quality of provision.

Strikingly, all of the practice leaders at the centre of the case studies were focusing on sharing practice leadership responsibility in order to broaden, deepen and/or sustain the improvements they had begun. Indeed, only one retained the formal designation of setting 'manager', although all were central in effecting change in their setting(s). The settings were at different stages in this process. Case study 1 focused on the distribution of practice leadership responsibility and resulted in the most dramatic improvements in the study. Case study 2 illustrated a setting at an earlier stage in the process, as a single practice leader attempted to turn rapid improvements into deeper, sustained change by sharing practice leadership. Case study 3 examined the impact of a practice leader working across three nurseries, where practice leadership had to be distributed to be most effective. And Case study 4 focused on the often undervalued challenge of maintaining high quality provision over time through building a shared understanding and culture of practice leadership.

Taken as a whole, the four case studies indicate how practice leaders addressed the challenges of improving the quality of provision by focusing explicitly on improving quality through building and extending their settings' capacity for practice leadership.

PART 3

6 Getting beneath the surface of improving quality

In the previous two chapters, we have set out how effective practice leaders improved the quality of provision in their settings by following four basic principles of practice:

- Assessing the gaps between the existing quality of provision and what they wanted to achieve.
- Using these gaps as a means of establishing common understandings of what requires improvement and what counts as improved practice.
- Designing a professional development programme to enhance practice leadership in key areas of improvement.
- Supporting the development of this emerging leadership capacity by linking individuals and building teams.

The previous chapters have tried to demonstrate how these principles play out in practice by drawing on leaders' accounts and case studies of different settings. These accounts and studies also demonstrate that the challenge facing these leaders was as much about how to enact these principles in their own settings as it was about understanding their importance in improving practice. These leaders displayed a fair degree of what might be described as 'situational awareness' or 'contextual literacy' in how and when they applied these four principles of practice.[1] But what does it mean to be contextually literate, or situationally aware? Surely all leaders have to have an understanding of the contexts in which they are working?

To an extent, as a strand of leadership activity, practice leadership requires no more or less intelligence or awareness than any other aspect of leadership. However, there are two features of practice leadership that need to be considered in more detail. In the majority of the case studies in the research, practice leadership was seen as a collaborative effort, based on the ability to build capacity for this aspect of leadership in a setting or settings. The collaborative and capacity building aspects of practice leadership require a nuanced form of situational awareness. First, it highlights the importance of understanding how to set up and monitor the kinds of feedback loops between existing and potential leaders discussed in Chapter 2. These loops ensured that, as leaders' activities helped to build greater capacity, the feedback they received changed how they subsequently worked with these emerging leaders. Their responses could range from adopting more distributed or collaborative approaches to leadership to focusing on new and more complex areas that required improvement. Managing and monitoring these feedback loops, recognising growth in leadership capacity and understanding how to respond to it, all are essential aspects of practice leaders' contextual literacy.

Second, as a collaborative process practice leadership requires what might be described as a 'stretched' form of situational awareness, a shared understanding of how the context is changing and how these changes allow for, and sometimes require, a very different form of leadership. Indeed, part of the capacity building activities of existing leaders is to develop this kind of shared understanding, particularly about the need to change how the setting was previously led and challenging ideas about who its leaders are and what constitutes leadership.

In this chapter, we set out a series of reflective tasks that can be used by both existing and emerging practice leaders to develop their contextual literacy. The chapter moves from helping individuals to understand and share aspects of their professional identities to considering the nature of leadership in a setting and how children's perspectives might be used to support practice leadership and quality improvement. In the process, we try and develop the idea that the context of a setting is not simply a given, it is a social construction that arises in large part from the actions and beliefs of the adults and children in the setting. Unwrapping the social constructions of others and how these shape the contexts in which we all work is a key part of developing contextual literacy.

Throughout this book, we have kept coming back to the idea of professional identity because it shapes what practitioners believe they should be doing and what they actually do. Helping individual practitioners to unpack aspects of their professional identity is useful both in increasing their self-awareness and also in helping them to explore the 'gaps' between what they think they should be doing and what they are actually achieving in practice. These gaps can in themselves become part of a reflective process that leads to further investigation and improvement. Processes and tools to support such investigations are set out in Chapter 7.

Task 6.1: Building your learning platform

A 'platform' is the basis on which you make professional judgements; it consists of numerous elements, including fundamental value positions, principles and general beliefs. At this level, the platform can be seen as part of the building blocks of your professional identity.[2] Reflecting on and articulating the principles and values that underpin your judgements is one way of understanding how you have constructed your professional identity and has a number of possible outcomes. It can build the confidence of emergent leaders by developing their self-awareness. It can help existing leaders understand the ideas and values with which practitioners interpret the innovations and evidence you present to them. It can also be an effective prompt for reflection on the gaps between what people would like to be doing and what they find themselves involved in on an everyday basis.

To help people articulate what can often be quite implicit ideas and support them in developing an appropriate vocabulary about learning and how it is developed, the platform activity is based on using metaphors and imagery. A platform is based on initially asking practitioners three or four fundamental but simple questions. In the following example (Figure 6.1) they were asked to draw their 'ideal' view of:

- *What is the child's role in learning?*
- *What is the adult's role in learning?*
- *What role should the environment play?*
- *What do leaders do to support learning?*

These images illustrate the values and beliefs of the practitioner who drew them, in which children's learning appears to be regarded as a complex

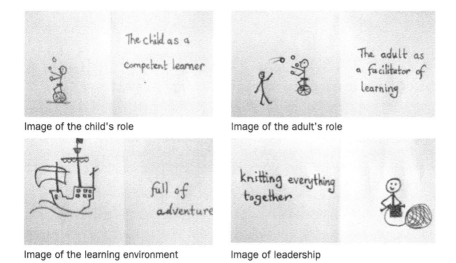

Image of the child's role   Image of the adult's role

Image of the learning environment   Image of leadership

Figure 6.1 Example images of practice.

juggling process wherein the practitioner's role is to support their development as autonomous learners rather than lead their learning directly. The learning environment is a scene of adventurous play, while the leader appears as orchestrator and coordinator, ensuring that the conditions are created that will enable the other images to come into being.

The next stage in the process would be for the practitioner to discuss these images with others or, if they are working on their own, to write a short paragraph about the meanings these images have for them. This process should help them start to develop their platform by bringing out key values and assumptions. Then they explore these images, talking about how closely they feel they can enact the values and beliefs they represent in their current setting. This discussion also provides opportunities to challenge these values and beliefs by comparing them to the images created by others or to the existing knowledge base around effective pedagogies.

After this, participants move from the ideal to the real by responding to the same four questions but drawing their 'actual' metaphors, based on their experiences in their current settings. Using metaphors in this way gets round individuals' reluctance to criticise current practice. Unpacking the images and metaphors is intended to articulate the experiences and evidence behind them. Finally, the process is developed further by exploring the gaps between the ideal and the actual. Here the discussion should be based on why participants think the gaps exist and what could be done to close them. The key point here is to help practitioners recognise that it may not be possible to achieve this in a single move. This should then lead to a discussion of possible next steps to improve practice. The overall purpose of the platform activity should be to support emergent practice leaders to develop their practice, in line with the values and beliefs that underpin their professional identities.

Task 6.2: Assessing your capacity for improvement

Our 30 case studies indicated how building capacity for improvement can take many forms, from formal professional development activities, such as mentoring, to using enquiry and modelling new practices. Developing an individual's situational awareness requires them to be able to make an assessment of the implications for current practice of any planned change, to assess the current capacity for improvement in the area, and to base their approaches to improvement on these judgements. The starting point for any innovation or improvement therefore needs to be some form of initial audit of existing practice and assessment of current capacity. This task introduces a basic format for doing this collectively with colleagues in your setting.

We recommend undertaking this reflective task as part of planning a change process collectively. It should help to develop shared understandings, awareness of training needs and the additional information needed either immediately or as the process develops. Start by marking out three rings on a large piece of paper (like in Figure 6.2) and encourage colleagues taking part to use Post-It® notes to write down suggestions for each level in turn, starting with their visions of the proposed change. Cluster similar ideas around the points identified in the circles, removing duplications or rejected suggestions as you finish each stage and adding things that the group feels have been missed. This process should help to develop shared understanding and help identify gaps in the team's knowledge at both individual and collective levels.

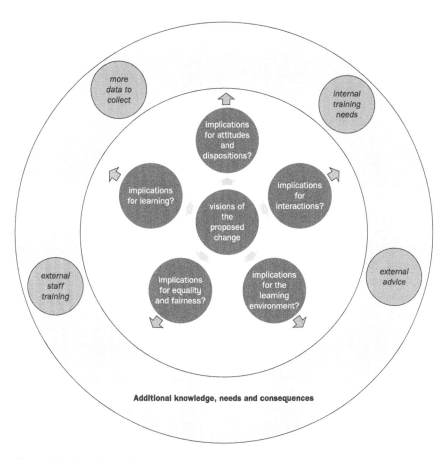

Figure 6.2 Capacity audit.

Task 6.3: Developing the capacity for improvement – using children's perspectives

When you think about capacity for improvement, what generally comes to mind are the skills and understanding of leaders and practitioners, but there are a range of others who can support improvement, including parents, carers and professionals in other agencies. One group of potential partners that is often overlooked is the children in the setting, who are often the focus of any improvement effort. This oversight arises from both technical concerns over how to include young children and broader issues about whether children should be included in direct discussions of the quality of their experiences.

We suggest that being able to draw on children's perspectives allows you to incorporate the views of those that matter most in the setting into the improvement process by exploring the change and the reasons for it. If effective consultation with stakeholders as a valuable means of involving them in the process of change and genuine consultation can make individuals feel empowered and engaged, then why would we not involve children?

Our research included a strand that focused on how practice leaders used children's perspectives in six settings.[3] The focus was on the ways in which practice leaders interested in promoting child-initiated learning were able to access and use children's perspectives in improving this aspect of their provision. We deliberately used the broad term 'children's perspectives' to incorporate aspects of child consultation, participation, children's voice and listening to children. Crucially, our approach involved listening attentively to the voice of the practice leader as well as to that of the child. We sought to explore how children's autonomy and agency were interpreted, and developed, in their settings. The process was carried out in partnership with practice leaders in the settings in order to investigate and promote the value of accessing and drawing on children's perspectives.

Some of the most advanced settings we worked with regarded consulting with children like this as an integral part of their work. Many shared Alderson's view that children are 'the primary source of knowledge about their own views and experiences'.[4] Alderson warned of the dangers of talking down to children or using language that they may find difficult to understand, but found that adults were often surprised by children's competence. This task is designed to support practitioners in involving children in the process of change. It is the starting point for helping you consider the ability of young children to become engaged in conversations and discussions about how to improve what happens in their setting and what role they could play in helping the setting improve.

The task begins by inviting two or three children to walk you around the setting and to talk about their favourite places and activities. They are then given cameras and invited to take photographs of some of these places and activities. These photographs are then used with these children, and others in the setting, as the basis of a reflective discussion, guided by the kinds of questions outlined below:

1   Tell me about the photos you've taken of your favourite places.
      Is that what you like doing best of all?
      Do you have enough time to do/play/use . . .?
      How does your mum/carer know what you do/like doing at nursery?
      Are there places where you don't feel comfortable/happy/safe?

2   Are there rules about the use of [photo]?
      Do you have different rules at home to nursery?
      What happens if children break the rules/do something wrong?
      What happens if the teacher tells you it's, say, lunchtime?

3   What happens if all the children are doing something and you want to do something different?
      Who do you talk to at nursery if something goes wrong/you are unhappy?

4   Are there any parts of the nursery you don't like?
      What things do you wish you didn't have to do?
      What happens if you say you don't like doing something?

These questions are only indicative. As you undertake this kind of process in your own setting, you will know how to pitch your questions appropriately for your children. This kind of approach will be familiar to many from the Mosaic approach, which uses multiple, child-friendly methods of enquiry to enable children to explore how they perceive the world and to communicate their ideas in a meaningful way.[5]

The next stage of the process is to work with the practitioner who has taken the lead in this task and to explore with him or her what they found surprising or challenging in the children's responses and in carrying out the process. As a one-off, this activity can challenge some practitioners' expectations about the role of children's perspectives in developing the quality of provision. However, to achieve sustained change it needs to be integrated into a setting's planning cycle.

Some of the settings we worked with had managed to integrate children's perspective work into their planning cycles, as illustrated in Figure 6.3, by ensuring that it formed part of the evaluative feedback used in assessing any major innovation.

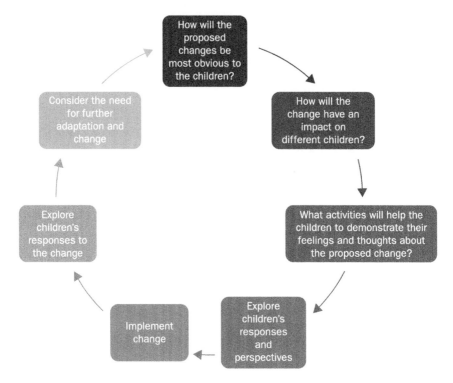

Figure 6.3 Integrating children's perspectives into reflective planning cycles.

Task 6.4: Assessing your practice leadership capacity

The previous task focused on a setting's current capacity in one area of improvement. This task will help you to consider the capacity for practice leadership in the same area. It is therefore a more finely-grained audit. Developing practice leadership capacity is a complex process. Encouraging a more collective or distributed leadership approach may generate opposition from colleagues, who may be unwilling to change their views of their own and their leaders' roles. This was identified as a problem by Lindon and Lindon who drew attention to how practitioners in some settings resisted colleagues stepping up to leadership roles and actively discouraged them from pursuing further studies or taking on additional responsibilities.[6]

This reflective activity is intended to help existing and emergent leaders reflect on what capacity for practice leadership they have in a specific area. Depending on whom you are working with, you may not want to take them through all the steps in the process. It is designed to help people identify the

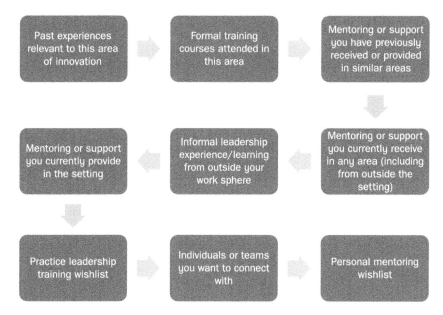

Figure 6.4   Practice leadership audit process.

various forms of leadership activities they have been involved in, including those outside their current context, and the sorts of support they would like to receive from current and emerging leaders. The process is an opportunity to unpick individuals' notions of what leadership is and who leads in a group or setting. In line with the themes in this book, it is therefore an opportunity to develop notions of collective leadership and the leadership of practice.

Each box in Figure 6.4 is a prompt for reflection if the task is being undertaken by an individual, or for discussion if it is done in groups. It can be undertaken in conjunction with Task 6.2 once that task has identified the capacity for change.

Task 6.5: Growing leadership capacity: mapping and nurturing relationships in your setting

This task has two functions. First, it is designed to help you identify current patterns of informal leadership and influence in your setting by mapping the professional relationships between colleagues in relation to a number of areas. Second, having mapped the relationships, it can help you nurture professional relationships to build the capacity to support your change agenda.

Developing and negotiating your leadership identity takes place dynamically as team identities are created and refined. As Chapter 4 indicated, some of the more effective settings in our research had established a philosophy of professional development that reflected their approach to child development. Practice leaders who did this successfully often had roles that connected managing improvements with overall responsibility for quality assurance and staff development. A key aspect of this role therefore was that they were able to integrate improvement efforts with professional development so that they reinforced each other across the setting.

Targeting professional development effectively requires you to know your colleagues well. This 'networking' task is intended to help you map key relationships in and between teams. It is based on the social network analysis technique we used in our research. As we outlined in more detail in Chapter 3, we asked all staff in a setting or, in some cases a group of settings, to name up to three people in response to the following kinds of questions:

- *Who are you most likely to talk to in the setting about your work with children?*
- *Who in the setting are you most likely to go to for reassurance and support about work-related issues?*
- *Which people in the setting do you go to for new ideas about improving practice in the setting?*
- *Who has mentored you at work in the last 12 months?*
- *Who have you gone to for advice or support about [a specific improvement focus] in the last 12 months?*

Whereas we used software to analyse the data collected from these surveys and create diagrammatic representations of the professional networks associated with these issues, you could undertake this task more quickly in a team meeting. You can simply gather participants' responses and immediately draw the kind of diagram illustrated in Figure 6.5,[7] which indicates the centrality of the support offered by the setting's leader and deputy. The questions included at the bottom of the diagram under the heading 'Identify' are prompts for subsequent discussion in the meeting. As well as quickly mapping the relationships in the setting, which can be done in a single diagram, as in Figure 6.5, or separately for each question, the diagrams will allow you subsequently to identify areas of the setting which require additional support or the nurturing of new relationships.

Identifying the support required is based on three questions, included at the bottom of Figure 6.5 under the heading 'Identify'. These are:

- *Who needs additional support?*
- *What sort of support do they need?*
- *Who could offer that support?*

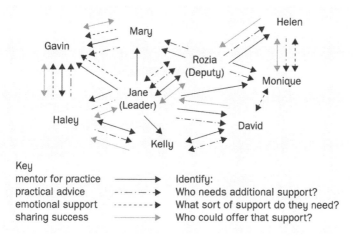

Figure 6.5 Mapping relationships in your setting.

These prompts can be used with the group as they complete their maps but can also be the subject of discussion by existing leaders as they consider how best to connect individuals and grow capacity.

Task 6.6: Growing leadership capacity: integrating formal and informal leadership structures

This task should be completed in conjunction with Task 6.5 and is based on the observation that in the most effective settings practice leaders worked to integrate established and informal leadership structures. This task can be undertaken by existing leaders after Task 6.5 has been completed to help them consider the implications of the emergence of new leadership capacity for their existing structures.

The task begins with the existing leaders drawing an organogram that indicates their current roles and responsibilities in their setting. These diagrams do not have to be too complicated and their focus can be refined by asking questions, such as:

- *What are our roles and responsibilities in terms of improving practice?*
- *What are our roles and responsibilities in terms of improving this area of our practice?*

Figure 6.6 is an example of a simple organogram drawn from one of the case studies in Chapter 5.

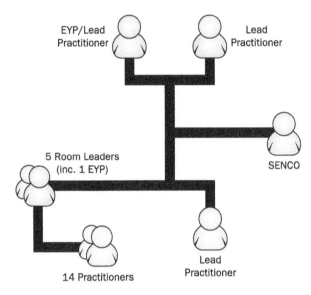

Figure 6.6 Example organogram.

Drawing these diagrams and discussing them can help clarify roles and responsibilities in relation to a specific area of practice or a particular intervention. The next stage is to compare this formal structure, and the roles and responsibilities it outlines, with existing support relationships. This comparison needs to be guided by a series of questions:

- *In what areas is there a good overlap between the formal roles and responsibilities and the informal support networks that have developed?*
- *Are there any areas where there is no, or limited, overlap between the formal roles and the informal support networks?*
- *How can we improve the overlap between the formal structure and the informal networks?*
- *How should we recognise someone's role in the informal network in the formal structure?*
- *What changes could we make to our existing leadership/meeting/planning structures so that existing leaders can become more central to the informal leadership structures?*
- *How can we change our existing leadership/meeting/planning structures to support the development of informal networks of support?*

The process of discussing and answering these questions will help you to compare formal and informal structures in your setting and identify emergent and potential leadership capacity.

Notes

1   See Southworth, G. (2004) *Primary School Leadership in Context: Leading Small, Medium and Large Sized Primary Schools*. London: Routledge Falmer; Spillane, J., Halverson, R. and Diamond, J. (2004) Towards a theory of leadership practice: a distributed perspective, *Journal of Curriculum Studies*, 36 (1), 3–34.

2   Hadfield, M. and Hayes, M. (1993) A metaphysical approach to qualitative methodologies, *Educational Action Research*, 1 (1), 153–74.

3   See Coleyshaw, L., Whitmarsh, J., Jopling, M. and Hadfield, M. (2012) *Listening to Children's Perspectives: Improving the Quality of Provision in Early Years Settings*. Research Report DFE-RR239b. London: DfE.

4   Alderson, P. (2008) Children as researchers: participation rights and research methods, in P. Christensen and A. James (eds.) *Research with Children: Perspectives and practices*, 2nd edn. London: Routledge, at p. 287.

5   See Clark, A. and Moss, P. (2001) *Listening to Young Children: The Mosaic Approach*. London: National Children's Bureau; Clark, A. and Moss, P. (2005) *Spaces to Play: More Listening to Young Children Using the Mosaic Approach*. London: National Children's Bureau.

6   Lindon, J. and Lindon, L. (2011) *Leadership and Early Years Professionalism: Linking Theory and Practice*. London: Hodder Education.

7   Needham, M. (2013) *Early Years Professionals as Targeted Mentors for Leadership and Study: A Qualitative Review of Practitioners' Experiences of a Pilot Project in Shropshire*. Wolverhampton: University of Wolverhampton.

7 Where to start in your setting

In Chapter 4, we described a model of practice leadership in action based on three stages of development: emergent, established and embedded. These stages were used to illustrate how settings in the research study moved from a situation where practice leadership was restricted in scope to one where it was recognised as a specific aspect of leadership, in which improving quality was the responsibility of a range of 'leaders'. Building a setting's capacity for practice leadership requires the development of sufficient practitioners who see themselves as having a leadership role that encompasses improving interactions between staff and children and bringing about sustained improvements in the learning environment. The complexity lies in how to achieve such a shift in practitioners' understanding of leadership and, if this is achieved, supporting these 'new' leaders to bring about change in others' practice. As those who have researched pedagogical, or instructional, leadership in schools have discovered, an individual's pedagogical approach is very closely tied to professional identity, including that person's views of how children learn and develop, and is constructed from complex sets of experiences that are influenced by the established cultural norms, practices and behaviours of individual schools or settings.[1]

Changes to any forms of established practice are difficult to achieve, especially when settings are conservative about what constitutes 'acceptable' practice, particularly if there are pressures from parents to maintain the status quo. Where there are few internal pressures to improve, it is usually external pressures, for example a poor inspection report or the introduction of a large-scale policy, such as the EYFS, that create an impetus for change. However, such external influences will be reinterpreted and reconstructed in settings through their existing internal cultural 'lens', reflecting one of the truisms of educational improvement that achieving effective change is technically simple but culturally complex.

Although we have a solid evidence base relating to effective leadership of pedagogical processes, there is no simple recipe that can be followed to ensure improvements are achieved. Rather, we need leadership approaches that are contextually intelligent and responsive to the possibilities and limitations of settings, as described in the case studies in Chapter 5. As Chapter 4 explored in depth, leadership in settings that managed to make substantive improvements in the quality of their practice focused their activities on four areas:

- strategically assessing the quality of current provision and relating this to an overall vision of quality;
- establishing a common understanding of improvements that were required and developing norms around quality;
- developing, leading and evaluating professional development activities that focused on improving process quality;
- enhancing practice leadership capacity in the setting by connecting individuals and building teams.

In this chapter, we discuss two broad categories of professional learning processes that can support practice leaders to develop their setting's capacity in each of these four key areas. The first category contains processes where **observation** is the basis for learning, examining practice in settings and reflecting on how it might be improved. The second category involves the **co-construction** of practice, planning, teaching and evaluation, and reflection on its successes and failures. In each category, we provide two examples: one that is more suitable for those working in settings where practice leadership is emerging and one for settings in which practice leadership is more established.

Both observations for learning and co-construction processes are based on approaches to professional learning that focus on improving the quality of the practical judgements being made in a specific context. Such judgements are not only technical – for example, based on evidence 'of what works' – they also often involve complex sets of moral, strategic and critical judgements. This is because they are inevitably affected by professional tensions and dilemmas about what can be achieved at that point, rather than what may be achievable in the future.[2] Leaders have to consider to what extent adopting a new set of practices constitutes a step nearer to the ultimate objective. Should you try to integrate different notions of quality and approaches to improvement? How do you weigh up the different impacts, both benefits and costs, of any new practices on all those involved? Reflecting on practical judgements and their outcomes is not simply about individuals reconstructing what has already occurred. It is both retrospective and prospective. Reflection that leads to improvements in practice leadership involves a social process of discussion and critique that encompasses both the 'what' and the 'how' of improvement. It is not enough for only the practice leader to recognise this. There has to come a point where all those who contribute to practice leadership in the setting share a commitment to achieving a set of working standards.[3]

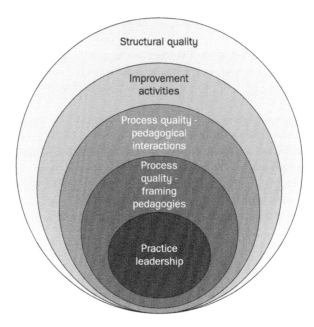

Figure 7.1 Practice leadership and improving quality in settings.

The following processes may be familiar to those of you who have been involved in professional development, but here they have been adapted specifically to support practice leadership learning in the early years. In adapting them, we have drawn on some of the key conceptual frameworks and tools we used in our research. Although they overlap, each process can be used to look at different aspects of the relationship between leadership, changing practice and improving quality. They are based on the model of practice leadership and quality improvement discussed in Chapter 2 and illustrated again in Figure 7.1.

Table 7.1 provides an overview of how the reflective learning processes, combined with these frameworks and tools, can be used to examine aspects of

Table 7.1 Overview of learning processes outlined in this chapter

Learning process	Aspects of quality	Capacity-building
Observations for learning		
Enquiry walkthrough	Process quality and structural quality	Emergent
Interactional rounds	Process quality – pedagogical interactions	Established
Co-construction		
Long table enquiry	Process quality – pedagogical interactions and framing pedagogies	Emergent
Learning Study	Process quality – pedagogical interactions	Established

quality and quality improvement. It also indicates the leadership capacity required to use the processes effectively. The nature and purpose of the tools are explained in the rest of the chapter.

Observations for learning

In this section, we introduce two types of observations of learning. The first, the enquiry walkthrough, is essentially a combination of a generic process with very specific observational tools – the ECERS and ITERS rating scales, which are used extensively in the early years sector.[4] The second draws on a very specific approach, instructional rounds, that has its own model of professional decision making and pedagogy. This approach has not commonly been used in the early years but here we present an adaptation, which we have called interactional rounds, that we believe will support practice leaders to focus their work on key aspects of early years pedagogy.

There are many variations of walkthroughs[5] and they have been used as everything from evaluation tools to being integrated into organisation-wide professional learning programmes. In common with many of the reflective processes discussed in this chapter, their origins can be traced back to early developments in action research and change management.[6] Walkthroughs in their simplest form are a series of observations of practice linked by conversations and feedback sessions relating to the observations. The observations and discussions are set within an overall enquiry process, with the focus agreed collaboratively by those undertaking the walkthrough and those being observed. In education, walkthroughs become highly structured processes when they are linked to specific pedagogical models or used to evaluate the fidelity of implementation of a particular intervention.[7]

Observation for learning 1: An enquiry walkthrough (emergent settings)

This process arises from our observation that many of the settings we studied were using established rating scales such as ECERS and ITERS to improve the quality of provision. However, in many instances they were used by those in formal leadership positions more as evaluation and accountability tools than as a means of building practice leadership capacity. This meant that, often, other practitioners were only included in the process at the point of feedback. This lack of involvement undermined some of the potentially most powerful aspects of such scales, that is, making explicit the notions of quality provision and pedagogical grounding that underpin them. Of greater concern was the fact that in certain settings the scales were being used in a very mechanistic way. In such instances, feedback to staff of 'their' ECERS or ITERS ratings resulted in them simply trying to ensure that they displayed practices that scored highest on each of the sub-scales without necessarily understanding why these constituted 'improved' practice. Such an approach could result in a narrowing repertoire of activities and limit innovation as practitioners adopt a fragmented notion of quality provision that lacks a secure theoretical underpinning.

An enquiry walkthrough can be used with any observation tool that identifies different aspects of effective practice. The benefit of using a rating scale is that they operationalise different aspects of practice and clarify what practitioners should observe. In the case of ECERS and ITERS, behaviours and environmental characteristics to be observed are arranged into sub-scales, which provide a great deal of support to those undertaking observations of practice. They have the advantage, for settings in which practice leadership has not been established, of facilitating wide-ranging discussion of the existing quality of provision and how it might be developed. Consequently, using this sort of tool can be very helpful when introducing walkthroughs, as they support and structure the reflective discussions that facilitate the development of practice leadership.

Designing an enquiry walkthrough

Whether you are going to walk one room in your setting or visit another setting, designing a walkthrough can essentially be broken down into three stages, as illustrated by Figure 7.2.

Purpose

Defining the purpose of your walkthrough will be based on your answers to the following questions:

- *Who do I want to influence?*
- *What aspect of their practice do I want to affect?*

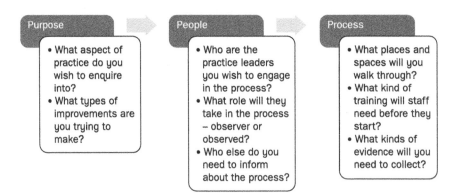

Figure 7.2   Stages of an enquiry walkthrough.

In this case, we are trying to build practice leadership capacity in a setting or settings by developing individuals' ability to assess the quality of current provision and consider the need for improvement. We are also trying to help individuals understand the role they can play in leading and supporting others. So the overarching purposes of this kind of enquiry walkthrough are:

- *To develop practitioners' ability strategically to assess the quality of current provision and establish a common understanding of required improvements.*
- *To enhance practice leaders' ability to support the professional learning of others via observation, feedback and engaging them in reflective discussions.*

To make this learning relevant and engaging, it needs to focus on a 'real', practical issue. The starting point for any enquiry is often a felt need or a 'professional itch' that requires scratching. It is always helpful to regard an enquiry walkthrough as a collaborative process, done with rather than to others and focused on shared issues. If a shared focus for practice improvement is not obvious, the practice leader organising the walkthrough may have to create one. Turning the issue or need identified into a question is a good starting point, because it draws people into the process and builds their willingness to learn. An enquiry walkthrough is likely to have one overall question, from which those involved may generate sub-questions with particular relevance to their areas of responsibility or interest.

Your starting point for generating the enquiry question will vary depending on your setting's current use of ECERS and ITERS. If you already use these scales, you will have developed a baseline profile for the setting that staff will already understand to some extent. This baseline, and shared understanding, could lead you on to consider enquiry questions such as:

- *Why do we see such different levels of quality between . . .?* or
- *What aspects of process quality should we focus on (drawing on the quality improvement model in Figure 2.12) . . .?*

If you or your colleagues have never used ECERS and ITERS before, a key aim of the enquiry walkthrough is to develop their use as a means of improving practice. You will have to introduce the frameworks gradually, so it makes sense to select the sub-scales that will be easiest to explore for those who are new to walkthroughs. This will probably mean beginning with aspects of the environment, rather than specific interactions.

Jointly select one or two sub-scales that you want to focus on within these areas. You might ask the following types of questions:

- *What would the highest quality provision in (insert one of the sub-scales) in our setting look like?* or
- *We'd like to find out more about how we approach (insert one of the sub-scales) in our setting?*

Once you have you identified the aspect of practice you wish to focus on, you need to list the spaces and practices associated with it in the setting. This may require sharing plans, timetables and accounts of staff development. This will give you an idea of what you would like to cover in the walkthrough and where and when it should take place.

People

Having decided on the purpose and focus of the enquiry walkthrough, it should now be clear whom you need to involve to ensure sufficient evidence is collected and that there are opportunities to discuss and feed back with those who have been observed. Settings with small numbers of staff will also require careful planning to maximise the number of staff involved. Although you can do a walkthrough on your own, the main benefits arise from the conversations you have about what has been seen and heard. Remember, a walkthrough need only last a few minutes, but the conversations around what was seen and heard should last much longer.

All the individuals involved will need to be briefed about the purpose of the walkthrough and their involvement. They may need to receive some training about the rating scales, using the videos explaining the scales or through a facilitated team training session, in order to familiarise themselves with their structure and application. However, at this stage the assessments themselves are not so important. The walkthrough process itself, during which participants discuss their ratings with others, will develop their ability to use the scales. Consequently, setting the tone for walkthrough is just as important as briefing the walkers and helping them familiarise themselves with the tools being used. The emphasis should be on learning, not accountability, and on trying to understand what is going on. This requires participants to adopt an appreciative, enquiring and non-judgemental mindset throughout, which can require strong leadership.

Process

All enquiries are informed by evidence, which is one of the key prompts in reflecting on the quality of practice and how it should be improved. The nature of the evidence you will collect will depend on the aspect of practice you are focusing on, but the ECERS and ITERS frameworks will be at the heart of this process. The first step in creating an evidence framework is to consider where and when you need to walk though in order to observe the interactions in which you are interested. Then you need to determine the basic forms of evidence to collect. Creating an evidence sheet, like that illustrated in Table 7.2, is one way of listing what you want to observe, see and read on a walkthrough.

Table 7.2 Evidence sheet

Reflections	See	Hear	Questions
	Read		

The **evidence sheet** is a summary, a reminder of the evidence you are interested in collecting. It is used during the walkthrough, but it is also a living document. The 'See' section will be the ECERS or ITERS sub-scales that are the focus of the walkthrough, but there may be other aspects of practice that you want to look at. The 'Hear' section will contain the interactions you might like to listen to and the people you want to talk to. The 'Read' section will contain documents, policies, and plans you would like to read. In the 'Questions' section, you list what you want to ask those you meet on the walkthrough, and the 'Reflections' section is for noting down thoughts about what you see and hear. Depending on your focus you may need to create other tools, besides ECERS and ITERS, for collecting and recording additional data. The next stage is to turn this series of tools and sources of data into a schedule for a walkthrough.

The **schedule** should make clear to all involved, including those being observed, which rooms are being walked and when. It should be clear who is going to talk to whom about what, in order to collect the evidence necessary to complete your evidence sheet. You will need to check the schedule with those being visited and clarify expectations about being observed or interviewed, such as obtaining the necessary permissions for photography or recording conversations.

The walkthrough will involve making observations and talking to staff and children, but you will also need to build in time for **debriefs** to reflect and discuss with others what you are finding out. This will involve you in discussing the ranking scale scores, your general observations and what you have drawn from the interviews. As these corridor conversations, or debriefs, are a form of ongoing analysis, and where most of the learning will take place, they need to be properly integrated into the schedule. Depending on how you have organised the walkthrough, these debriefs can take place at various points. You might hold a debrief after each observation, or use coffee breaks and lunchtimes. If they take place part of the way through the walkthrough, they obviously need to be tentative, but this will help re-direct the enquiry towards emerging issues and develop shared understandings. Debriefs need to be based on issues and observations such as:

- *It was interesting when . . .*
- *I'm wondering . . .*
- *I'd like to know more about . . .*
- *I'd like to understand more about . . .*
- *What I'm struck by is . . .*

It is important to provide verbal feedback to those who are observed during the walkthrough as soon as possible afterwards. This should also be planned into your schedule. This feedback should be framed by the same type of questions and observations as the debriefs are. They are an opportunity to carry on your discussions about what is happening in the setting, based on your observations.

Finally, the walkers need to have an opportunity to **share their thoughts and insights** and revisit the issues and questions that originally framed the walkthrough. If you are using ECERS and/or ITERS or a similar tool, the rating scale should be the starting point for the discussions and for any summative feedback. The discussion of each aspect of the sub-scale should initially focus on the evidence you considered when making your judgement. Discussing evidence should highlight differences between what was observed and the ways in which the walkers interpreted it using the scales. Only at this point should the discussion move on to the actual rating scores and attempts to reach a consensus about the quality of current practice and which areas need to be improved. Focusing on improvements should provide an opportunity for a wider discussion of what counts as 'better' practice and the ideas and evidence on which this is based. During the final part of this session, the walkers draw up their main observations and insights and decide how these should be communicated back to those who have been visited. The emphasis should not be on feeding back the rating scores but rather on comments and questions that will prompt reflection on practice. The walkers should carry out a brief evaluation of the process itself and this should feed forward into the planning of any subsequent walkthroughs.

Observation for learning 2: Interactional rounds (established settings)

'Instructional rounds' is a term made popular by City et al. (2009).[8] It is derived from medical rounds, during which novice doctors are trained by consultants to diagnose patients and recommend treatments. In an ideal round, the consultant acts as both mentor and coach while junior doctors solve problems collaboratively and share their expertise. The model of decision making used in rounds emphasises the dangers of rushing to judgement or diagnosis and breaks the process down into four stages:

- Describe what is observed
- Analyse any patterns that emerge
- Predict the kind of outcomes that might be expected from what has been observed
- Recommend the next level of practice[9]

Instructional rounds in education focus not on diagnosing patients but on a problem or a practice, like the felt need that is the starting point for many enquiries. For problems of practice to be the focus of an instructional round, they need to be observable in the setting and something that people can learn about through observation.

The pedagogical change model on which rounds are based fits with this need to be observable. It focuses on what is called the 'instructional core', which, as Figure 7.3 indicates, consists of the interactions between the teacher, the learner and the content of the lesson. From this perspective, there are only three ways to improve provision: change the content, change the teaching approach, or change the way children engage. As the model is based on the proposition that each element of the core interacts with the others, changing one of them will affect the other two. In the rounds process, the instructional core is the lens through which classrooms are observed and the framework for analysing what was learned from these observations. Basically, if you cannot see 'learning' in the core, then it is not taking place.

With a few minor alterations to the concepts and ideas that underpin the process, instructional rounds can be adapted to work in the early years sector. The reason for making this effort is that, as an observational process, rounds can focus on key aspects of effective early years pedagogy. The key issue is ensuring that the round is an opportunity for joint observations, discussion and shared decision making among practitioners, which address pressing practical issues in settings.

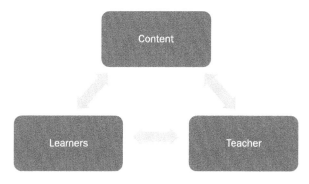

Figure 7.3 The instructional core.

The instructional core is a slightly more problematic model to apply to early years than enquiry walkthroughs because of the terminology used and its focus on instruction and curriculum content. Fundamentally, the model is used as a lens to focus observations on what is core to learning. The model expresses its developers' 'theory of action', what they see as the causal links between what practitioners do as teachers and how children learn. As they discuss in groups what they have observed, analyse what they have seen and predict what they think the outcomes will be for children, using the instructional core as a reflective framework, they are effectively articulating their own theories of action and examining those of others. The key question is how this 'core' can be developed to help early years practitioners articulate their theories of action.

From instruction to interaction

In our research, we were greatly influenced by the REPEY project's three-part model of pedagogy that is made up of adult and child involvement, cognitive (co-constructive) engagement and the use of instructional techniques. At the general level, the instructional core could address all the aspects of this pedagogical model but, as it is currently constructed, it tends to focus on instructional techniques such as modelling, demonstrating, questioning and providing feedback. Although these are important aspects of quality provision, much of the emphasis in the early years is on practitioner and child interactions, particularly those related to extending thinking. This emphasis on interactions derives from the EPPE study, which associated extending thinking with high quality teaching and positive learning outcomes for young children, as Chapter 1 highlights. This was subsequently integrated into policy initiatives such as the EYFS in England, underlining the fact that interaction between practitioners and children, rather than instruction, is at the core of early years pedagogy. In particular, cognitive engagement that leads to co-construction of meaning and understanding, such as sustained shared thinking, has been associated with long-term positive outcomes for children. Such engagement comes from interactions where two or more individuals (children together, or adults and children) work together to solve a problem, clarify a concept, evaluate activities or extend a narrative.[10] This led us to approach early years pedagogy in terms of an 'interactional core', as Figure 7.4 illustrates.

In adapting instructional rounds for use in early years, we believe that we need to take the tradition of observation in the sector and focus it on this interactional core. A number of existing tools are available to help us do this. In our research, we developed an observational instrument, the Practitioner Child Interaction Tool (PCIT), which amalgamated two existing tools to help us observe interactions between adults and children and thus this pedagogical core. In order to assess the general quality of interactions, we used a simplified version of the Adult Engagement Scale developed by Pascal and Bertram

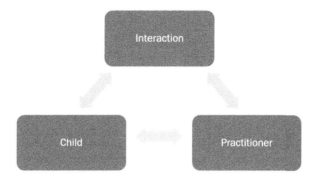

Figure 7.4 The interactional core.

(1997).[11] The PCIT was divided into a number of categories, two of which are illustrated in Table 7.3. The first category of sensitivity was included because of the emphasis placed in REPEY on the need for adults to be sensitive to children's intentions and meaning in order to foster learning. The second category of autonomy reflects the importance placed on child-initiated play and activity. Observations are typically undertaken for a period of 20–30 minutes, during which the interaction is given a rating, at two-minute intervals, of between 1 and 5 for sensitivity and autonomy. These can be averaged and compared across observations, or examined for fluctuations. The PCIT also recorded elements of interactions that might generate co-construction, specifically those that might provide opportunities for sustained shared thinking. These can be recorded as frequency counts, drawing on the elements used in the REPEY observation tools[12] and their subsequent development in further research. Examples of what to look for in relation to sustained shared thinking are outlined in more detail in Appendix 2.

The PCIT is only one of a number of tools that can help focus observations on the interactional core during a round.[13] However, care needs to be taken that their use does not overwhelm, or even replace, the discussion of participants' theories of action. They are only an aid, a more focused lens to help practitioners to understand their own and others' approaches and their outcomes in practice.

If both the approach to making professional judgements and the underpinning pedagogical model can be adapted to the early years sector, can the process be applied as well? First of all, the idea of rounds is based on collaborative learning in and between schools. Inter-visitations and networking are much more established approaches to improvement in the schools sector than in early years. Adopting this approach in the early years would require not only a shift in culture, but also overcoming considerable practical problems to allow groups of practitioners to carry out rounds in their own setting, never

Table 7.3 Assessing the quality of interactions (taken from PCIT)

Quality of interaction	Observation	5	4	3	2	1	Quality of interaction
HIGH SENSITIVITY: The adult • Is warm and demonstrates affection; • Makes positive body gestures & eye contact; • Praises effort & achievement, respects & values the child; • Empathises with the child's needs & concerns; • Listens to & responds to the child & includes child in discussion.	2 min 4 min 6 min 8 min 10 min 12 min 14 min 16 min 18 min 20 min						LOW SENSITIVITY: The adult • Is cold and distant; • Praises indiscriminately; • Puts the child down, criticises & rejects; • Confirms failure; • Does not empathise with child's needs & concerns; • Lacks responsiveness & does not listen; • Speaks to others about child as if child is not there.
HIGH AUTONOMY: The adult • Encourages child to be responsible for their actions; • Facilitates self-management & empowerment of the child; • Enables child to choose & supports child-initiated ideas; • Provides opportunities for experimentation; • Encourages child to bring their activity to a natural conclusion; • Encourages the child to negotiate. Conflict and rules.	2 min 4 min 6 min 8 min 10 min 12 min 14 min 16 min 18 min 20 min						LOW AUTONOMY: The adult • Dominant or 'laissez-faire'; • Takes responsibility rather than enabling child to take responsibility; • Gives child no room for choice or experimentation; • Allows no negotiation; • Disempowers & restricts self-management of the child; • Rigidly enforces rules & routines.

mind other settings. The other main issue is that the rounds require strong facilitation, not least because the 'problems of practice' that are the starting points for the rounds need to arise out of a gap between settings' improvement aspirations and what they are achieving in practice. This also has to relate to an area of the instructional, or interactional, core that is observable. Selecting an appropriate focus for a round therefore requires a good understanding of the 'failures' of a setting, the idea of the core, and some expertise in supporting others to make observations. This is why this process is recommended for settings in which practice leadership is already established.

Figure 7.5 Interactional rounds process.

Overall, the rounds process is not significantly different from the walk-through approach discussed previously. It consists of the four stages outlined in Figure 7.5.

The problem of practice

A problem of practice is something a setting cares about, feels stuck on and wants to understand more deeply. Selecting an appropriate problem of practice for an instructional round is key. It needs to be:

- an aspect of effective practice, which, despite all efforts, is still not established;
- observable in classrooms;
- something that the enquiry team can learn more about from observation.

What kind of practice problems might we come across in the early years sector? If we start to consider a 'gap' between what is aspired to and what is achieved in practice, in England we might look to the EYFS and ask ourselves which aspects of practice in the setting still fall short of its recommendations. The problems of practice that might arise from attempts to implement the EYFS could include:

- *Are staff getting the right balance between child-initiated and prac-titioner-led activities?*
- *How is space created for the children to control some activities so that they can learn to manage their own thinking and learning?*
- *Are staff able to develop opportunities for sustained shared thinking?*
- *How are the adult's interactions matched to the children's interests so as to provoke learning?*
- *Are staff promoting positive learning dispositions as well as specific skills and knowledge?*

Observation of practice

The observation of practice would start with the facilitator of the round setting out the problem to focus on. The use of an observational tool such as the PCIT would help focus observations on the nature of the interactions

Table 7.4 Observation sheet

What is the problem of practice?	
What were the adults saying and doing?	What were the children saying and doing?
What tasks were the children involved in?	

occurring in the room and particularly the way in which practitioners shape these interactions. If this is initially seen as too detailed, a more simple observation tool can be created using the interactional core as a framework. For each observation, a very basic sheet like the one illustrated in Table 7.4 could be created that merely focuses on what is being said or done in the room or setting in which the problem of practice is located.

Learning from practice

The mantra that underpins the rounds process is:

- **Observation before analysis** – Describe what you saw and heard
- **Analysis before prediction** – Analyse what the descriptive evidence means
- **Prediction before evaluation** – Predict what the children are actually learning

This is aimed at ensuring that there is no rush to judgement or intervention. The process for learning from the practice that has been observed therefore has to follow a number of discrete steps. First, it requires each individual walker to look through their observations and draw out from these notes what they regard as the most significant aspects of practice relating to the problem that is the focus of the walk. They will also need to be warned that they might have to justify these decisions later to all the walkers. Then, the walkers come together as a group and begin to share their most significant observations. Once these have been identified, they can start to group them and consider the following questions:

- Are any patterns of practice emerging?
- What insights have the observations given us about our problem of practice?

The next stage requires the walkers to consider what impact these practices might be having on children's learning and how this might be improved. The rationale for asking practitioners to make predictions is not just the quest for possible solutions but also the process of group reflection that aims to help those involved to articulate their theories of action about the interactional core. Put simply, it helps them describe the hypotheses relating to the link between practice and learning that underpin their work, such as 'If children and practitioners are involved in interaction X and having discussions that are marked by Y, then are children likely to learn X?' The question the group needs to be asking at this point is, 'If you were a child in that room and you were having the types of interactions you observed, what would you be learning?' This process of predicting outcomes from current practice should lead them to consider what needs to be changed in order to overcome the problem of practice and to suggest improvements that move them on to thinking about next practice.

Moving to next practice

The improvement model that underpins rounds is based on the idea that they will be repeated in cycles. At this point in the round, the walkers have started to generate a series of ideas about how they might tackle the problem of practice. These are likely to vary from concrete suggestions to questions that might require additional rounds. Here, it is the role of the facilitator to shape the next steps for the setting. If it is still unclear as to what should be done, the next step might be a more focused round. If there is a fair degree of confidence in the suggested improvements, an action plan can be developed to establish who will be involved and the time frames for the activities. At this point, the evaluation of any new innovation will have to be planned, and built into the ongoing cycle of rounds.

Co-construction of new practice

Observations can provide a rich source of joint reflection on the nature of practice. By generating discussion they can also support practitioners to articulate their theories of action and build consensus around the current nature of provision and new ways of working. The co-construction of new practices has many of these advantages with the additional benefit of being disruptive in the positive sense that any innovation will challenge existing norms and expectations by modelling new ways of working. This ability to disrupt is important in settings where there is resistance to change. Freeing a 'stuck' organisation often involves breaking down habits and routines that have been applied excessively or inappropriately.

In this section, two co-constructive processes are discussed. The first is the long table enquiry, a means by which practice leaders can share innovations with colleagues. As a process it is well suited to settings with low levels of leadership capacity, as it initially only requires one practitioner to have the confidence to innovate and then share their work with others. The second process, Learning Study, is a more challenging approach to co-construction in that it requires pairs or groups of individuals to work together on new practices at the same time.

Co-construction 1: Long table enquiry (emergent settings)

A long table enquiry is a way of reconstructing the process an individual has gone through as they have carried out an innovation. The purpose of a long table conversation is to explore the journey travelled by those involved. The process is based on the idea of stimulated recall,[14] but rather than using audio or video recordings of someone's practice to stimulate reflections on their 'in-flight' decision making, these long table enquiries use artefacts to help innovators reflect on and articulate how they managed to change their practice and innovate over time. These long table enquiries were part of the methodology used in our research in the case study settings as they helped practice leaders retrospectively to reconstruct their approach to improving aspects of practice. The long table enquiry process is very flexible; it can be carried out by two people over a lunch break or involve all the staff in a setting for part of a professional development day. What is crucial, however, is that the process is tightly structured in order to generate professional learning.

Preparing for a long table enquiry

A long table enquiry is essentially a retrospective, collaborative exploration of a mature innovation. What is being co-constructed is not the innovation *per se*, but a shared understanding of why the innovation was undertaken, how it was developed over time and the key professional judgements that shaped it. To co-opt the language of instructional rounds, it is a conversation that starts with the innovator's theory of action in order to support participants to reflect on their practice.

The long table enquiry starts with any innovation in the setting that focuses on an aspect of practice requiring improvement. At the outset, this innovation may not have been undertaken collaboratively, it might simply have involved the practice leader modelling practice that they wish to see embedded in the setting. As the innovation rolls out, it is important to archive evidence of what has been occurring. For example, we encouraged our case study participants to keep a journal in which they recorded their reflections on the issues and areas they were leading, in terms of both successes and failures. The artefacts are there to stimulate reflection from the innovator and everybody else taking part in the enquiry. It is therefore helpful to choose artefacts that will stimulate their thinking about the whole process. This means keeping examples of planning materials, children's work, observational notes, possibly photographs and videos, and the outcomes of any evaluative processes. These should help portray the development and implementation of the initiative. The idea is to create an evidential timeline of the whole innovation from inception to evaluation to capture its impact on practice. To avoid overloading the process with too much data, we recommend using only six to eight artefacts. They should be regarded as prompts for reflection rather than as a complete evidence base of what occurred.

Engaging in a long table enquiry

Obviously, it is important to find a room big enough to allow everyone involved in the enquiry to move around the table on which the artefacts are placed. The enquiry is best done standing, so that all the participants can walk up and down the table with you. The long table is a way of both spreading out the artefacts and creating a space in which colleagues can focus their discussion on the artefacts in front of them. The size of the table is determined as much by the size of the group involved as the number and nature of the artefacts. If you use video or audio recordings, they can either be placed on the table or symbolically represented and played separately. The artefacts need to be moved around to create a timeline for the innovation; you can even physically show the timing of events by using cards or Post-Its®.

There are two separate and distinctive roles to be played in the process. Normally, the innovator will be the host enquirer, as they are the person who has invited the others to enquire into an aspect of their practice by assembling the collection of artefacts. The others are the co-enquirers who will be asked to lead the innovator through a series of conversations about what shaped their work. If you, as practice leader, are the host enquirer, you will need to explain the process to the co-enquirers before you begin and probably keep reminding them of the stages and protocols. If you are not the innovator, you can act as a facilitator throughout the process. The key is for the co-enquirers gradually to take more and more responsibility for the process. They need to be actively engaged in trying to understand what the innovator has been doing, rather than passively being told 'how they did it'.

Having laid the artefacts out on the table, the enquiry follows a series of steps:

Step 1: The first step is for the co-enquirers to take the host through the steps of the enquiry and set the tone for what is going to happen. That means reassuring them that the process is enquiring and reflective, not judgemental, and should be mutually beneficial.

Step 2: The host should lead the co-enquirers through each of the artefacts, describing the journey by explaining what each artefact represents. The co-enquirers should at this stage simply listen and make notes without interrupting the flow of the account. This process should be seen as an informal, 'thinking aloud' process, rather than a presentation. In preparing for this journey, some of the things the host might consider are:

- *Why was this a priority for you or the setting?*
- *What thinking went into each of the stages?*
- *What were the key decisions and why were those choices made?*
- *What were the challenges and how were they overcome?*
- *What do you do differently now?*
- *What difference has it made (and how do you know)?*
- *What do you think the next steps might be?*

Step 3: This is an opportunity for the co-enquirers to ask clarifying questions of the host. These should be questions about things that are unclear, perhaps an acronym they do not recognise or phraseology with which they are unfamiliar. It is not the right point for questions about the substance of the presentation.

Step 4: The co-enquirers should now take time to study the artefacts, continuing to make notes and drawing the host into conversations about the detail behind what has been presented. The language of those conversations should be inquisitive, using the following kinds of questions:

- *What do you mean by . . .?*
- *How did you . . .?*
- *What happened when . . .?*
- *What were . . .?*

Step 5: At this point, the co-enquirers start a conversation with the host about what they are learning. The first part of the conversation should be an opportunity to share the things they have heard which they have found useful. The second part of the conversation should move to questions the process has prompted for their own practice. The third part of the conversation is a chance for the host to share where their thinking has moved to as a result of this particular practice, and what has come out for them from the long table enquiry.

If people are new to the process, you can provide more structure by asking the co-enquirers to complete the grid illustrated in Table 7.5 as they move through the enquiry.

Co-construction 2: Learning Study (established settings)

Learning Study is an adaptation of Lesson Study, which originated in Japan where it is widely used. It was brought to worldwide attention by the Third

Table 7.5 Notes from a long table enquiry

What was the artefact?	Why was this seen as key?	What professional judgements were discussed at this point?	On what basis did they make these judgements?	Do you have any concerns or other things you want to know?

International Trends in Mathematics and Science Study.[15] Since then, Lesson Study has been applied to a broad range of curriculum areas and has been applied and re-interpreted in a number of professional development programmes globally.[16] Western interpretations of the process have varied considerably from the original Japanese conception in that they have tended to focus on shorter-term and more measurable learning outcomes than the longer-term, more holistic objectives of the original process.

At the heart of the Learning Study process is a group of practitioners working together to help one another improve a particular area of their practice. Together they design innovative approaches in their area of focus, observe one another using the new ideas, then critique and refine it and teach it again. This should be a safe place to take risks and solve problems relating to pedagogy or interactions. It is about asking questions about how we teach, and interact with, children and how this affects the learning that occurs, rather than about the content of a lesson or session.

How then might Learning Study be useful in building practice leadership capacity in the early years? First, we have moved away from the notion of the 'lesson', with its connotations of school and timetables, to focus on 'learning episodes' and to return to the more holistic notions contained in the original Japanese lesson study. To reflect this, we have modified its name to 'Learning Study' to make it more appropriate to the early education context. The original aim was often to look at the development of 'a big idea in a very small way'. This would typically combine a broad educational aim with a specific aspect of the curriculum. So, for example, we might want to consider how to make children more independent as they explore mark making or look at how to make learning more enjoyable as children share a story. It is this tension between a big idea and making it come alive in a very specific practice that lies at the heart of the learning that results from involvement in a Learning Study. The approach is holistic in that it recognises that, in any learning episode, as well as having specific learning objectives, we are also involved in developing social, behavioural and attitudinal outcomes, modelling metacognitive (learning to learn) skills and reinforcing and applying prior learning and skills.[17] This holistic approach ensures that those involved ask themselves big pedagogical questions as they work on very specific interactions with children.

A focus on pedagogical interactions is the key to improving the quality of early years provision. In a Learning Study, the focus needs to be informed by research into effective pedagogical practices. The early years sector is fortunate in having some of the most robust research in this area. If we were to start simply with the findings from the Researching Effective Pedagogy in the Early Years (REPEY) study,[18] we could easily identify a range of 'big ideas', as well as how these need to be introduced, such as the following:

- Effective pedagogy is both 'teaching' and the provision of instructive learning and play environments and routines.
- The most effective settings provide both teacher-initiated group work and freely chosen yet potentially instructive play activities.
- Excellent settings tend to achieve an equal balance between adult-led and child-initiated interactions, play and activities.
- The most highly qualified staff provide the most direct teaching alongside the kind of interactions which guide but do not dominate children's thinking.
- Teachers stimulate children's activity and talk through 'sustained shared thinking'.

Designing a Learning Study

The overall flow of a Learning Study is similar to the other processes that have been described in this section, but with a number of key characteristics. Generally, a Learning Study contains the following elements:

- A shared goal – this might be described as a research focus, theme or aim.
- A focus on learning in a particular content area – this could be a weakness in an area of pedagogical interactions or an aspect of learning.
- Careful study of children learning – evidence is gathered on how children learn, engage and interact with others.
- The planning of study (or research) lessons/sessions by the group.
- Live observations of study lessons/sessions by members of the group (usually with a member of the group teaching). Although this may be supplemented by other forms of data, immersion in the teaching context is seen as important in understanding the complexity of practitioner–child interaction.
- Some form or plenary or review of the session by those who have taught and co-planned it.
- Passing on knowledge of what has been learned to others – through a 'public research lesson' open house or through presenting the

outcomes to colleagues more formally in written papers or presentations.[19]

The key characteristics of Learning Study are that it requires a team approach, preferably with practitioners working in threes or more, but pairs working closely together are also possible. This is because there is a requirement not only to observe children's learning and practitioners' interactions directly, but also to allow for team teaching approaches to be used when trying an innovation. If this approach is adopted, one of the investigators will work with a small group of children to try the innovation, while the others observe and work with the rest of the children. The team can decide whether they all test the innovation, rotating roles as necessary, or allow one of them to try it before others replicate it.

To assist with the close observation of learning and pedagogical interactions, the focus is on a small sample of children. Unless the focus of the Lesson Study requires otherwise, the sample should be broadly representative of the whole group in terms of ability and disposition towards learning. Focusing on the responses of this small group of learners during the observation of practice means the observer can capture more detailed data. If a team approach to introducing the new practices is adopted, then these children may also be the group the team works with. The focus on a small group plays a key role in making the process a safe place in which to innovate. The team approach and initial focus on a small group of children allows the pedagogical innovation being introduced to be a bespoke design, based on close observations of this group and their approach to learning. This is important in developing the investigators' approach to task design and assessing children's learning and evaluation. The discussions after observing how the innovation went with this smaller group, and to what extent it is more widely applicable, provide opportunities for exploring key pedagogical issues, such as how to differentiate the degree of cognitive challenge children face.

The final key characteristic is that the investigators make a commitment to share their learning with others. This may be through the use of a 'public research lesson' which colleagues are invited to observe, through using a long table enquiry as discussed earlier, or through the development of some form of professional development activity, possibly using videos of the sessions that were observed. Whatever approach is adopted, it needs to present the somewhat messy reality of innovation while clearly setting out the rationale behind the chosen focus, the evidence that was used, the way in which the innovation was designed, and the investigators' reflections on its impacts on children and practitioners.

The fact that the focus of the Learning Study needs to be holistic, related to pedagogical interactions and informed by research, means that this process is best used in settings in which practice leadership is established. It requires practice leaders not only to provide a connection to the existing evidence base, but also to create a space for co-design and peer-to-peer observation. As Learning Studies are not primarily concerned with content, they have the potential to encourage collaboration between practitioners working with children of different ages in a setting about how best to develop the same attitudes, skills and dispositions across different age groups of children.

Notes

1 See Spillane, J.P., Diamond, J.B. and Jita, L. (2003) Leading instruction: the distribution of leadership for instruction, *Journal of Curriculum Studies*, 35 (5), 533–43; Hallinger, P. (2003) Leading educational change: reflections on the practice of instructional and transformational leadership, *Cambridge Journal of Education*, 33 (3), 329–51; Harris, A. and Muijs, D. (2005) *Improving Schools through Teacher Leadership*. Maidenhead: Open University Press.

2 See Hadfield, M. and Hayes, M. (1993) A metaphysical approach to qualitative methodologies, *Educational Action Research*, 1 (1), 153–74; Sergiovanni, T.J. and Carver, F.D. (1980) *The New School Executive: A Theory of Administration*, 2nd edn. New York, NY: Harper & Row; and, for what may be achievable in the future, Day, C. and Hadfield, M. (1996) Effectiveness and quality in continuing professional education: an empirical investigation of policy and practice in UK universities, *International Journal of Lifelong Education*, 15 (5), 370–81.

3 See Whalley, M. (2008) *Leading Practice in Early Years Settings (Achieving EYPS)*. Exeter: Learning Matters.

4 See Harms, T., Clifford, R. and Cryer, D. (1998) *Early Childhood Environment Rating Scale* (revised edn.). New York, NY: Teachers College Press; Harms, T., Cryer, D. and Clifford, R.M. (2003) *Infant/Toddler Environment Rating Scale – Revised*. New York, NY: Teachers College Press; Sylva, K., Siraj-Blatchford, I. and Taggart, B. (2003) *Assessing Quality in the Early Years: Early Childhood Environment Rating Scale-Extension (ECERS-E): Four Curricular Subscales*. Stoke-on Trent: Trentham Books.

5 See Kachur, S., Stout, J. and Edwards, C. (2013) *Engaging Teachers in Classroom Walkthroughs*. Alexandria, VA: ASCD.

6 Adelman, C. (1993) Kurt Lewin and the origins of action research, *Educational Action Research*, 1 (1), 7–24.

7 See Goldman, P., Resnick, L., Bill, V., Johnston, J., Micheaux, D. and Seitz, A. (2004) *Learning Walk Source Book*. Pittsburgh, PA: Learning Research and Development Center.

8 City, E., Elmore, R., Fiarman, S. and Teitel, L. (2009) *Instructional Rounds in Education: A Network Approach to Improving Teaching and Learning*. Boston, MA: Harvard Education Press.

9 See Blanding, M. (2009) Treating the 'instructional core': education rounds. *Usable Knowledge*, 12 May. Cambridge, MA: Harvard Graduate School of Education.

10 See Siraj-Blatchford, I. (2009) Conceptualising progression in the pedagogy of play and sustained shared thinking, *Educational and Child Psychology*, 26 (2), 77–89.

11 Pascal, C. and Bertram, T. (1997) *Effective Early Learning: Case Studies in Improvement*. London: Hodder & Stoughton.

12 See Siraj-Blatchford, I., Sylva, K., Muttock, S., Gilden, R. and Bell, D. (2002) *Researching Effective Pedagogy in the Early Years*. Research Report DFES-RR356. London: DfES.

13 For alternatives, see Laevers, F. (ed.) (1994) *Well-being and Involvement in Care Settings: A Process-oriented Self-evaluation Instrument*. Leuven: Research Centre for Experiential Education, University of Leuven; or Pascal, C., Bertram, A.D., Ramsden, F., Georgeson, J., Saunders, M. and Mould, C. (1996) *Evaluating and Developing Quality in Early Childhood Settings: A Professional Development Programme*. Worcester: Amber Publications.

14 See Calderhead, J. (1981) Stimulated recall: a method for research in teaching, *British Journal of Educational Psychology*, 51 (2), 211–17.

15 TIMSS (1998) *Third International Trends in Mathematics and Science Study*. New Zealand: Comparative Education Research Unit.

16 See, for example, Lewis, C., Perry, R. and Hurd, J. (2004) A deeper look at lesson study, *Educational Leadership*, 61 (5), 18–23; Chokshi, S. and Fernandez, C. (2004) Challenges to importing Japanese lesson study: concerns, misconceptions, and nuances, *Phi Delta Kappan*, 85 (7), 520–5; Dudley, P. (2012) Lesson study in England: from school networks to national policy, *International Journal for Lesson and Learning Studies*, 1 (1), 85–100.

17 See Carr, M. and Lee, W. (2012) *Learning Stories: Constructing Learner Identities in Early Education*. London: Sage.

18 Siraj-Blatchford et al. (2002).

19 Perry, R.R. and Lewis, C.C. (2009) What is successful adaptation of lesson study in the US?, *Journal of Educational Change*, 10 (4), 365–91.

Postscript: The future of practice leadership

We began this book by discussing how practice leadership as a strand of leaders' activities had become increasingly important because of the overlapping concerns and interests of policy makers, researchers and practitioners. It remains a contested space in which these overlapping concerns are played out. Policy makers are focused on defining what constitutes quality provision and ensuring that minimum standards are met, while requiring that it can withstand international comparisons and resonate with their own political and ideological interests. For researchers in the early years, as with many other education researchers, the focus on what constitutes effective practice in terms of ensuring better outcomes for children has led to the development of causal chains linking leaders' activities to pedagogical improvements in settings. Finally, working in a sector where their sense of professionalism is under scrutiny and their status as professionals is increasingly being defined and measured against set standards, practitioners have found themselves caught between a desire to express their own values and beliefs about quality and the recognition that their settings remain subject to the scrutiny of external inspection regimes. Thus, this space is characterised by a range of voices, different forms of evidence, and diverse theories, all engaged in defining quality provision and how to achieve it in practice. In this final section, we want briefly to consider the future of practice leadership in relation to policy, what leaders do in practice, and leadership theory and research.

Policy and practice leadership

A good starting point is to consider what happened to Early Years Professional Status (EYPS) in England, the focus of our research and one of the more clearly articulated policies which has delineated what practice leaders should be involved in. The policy agenda in England has moved on and, in 2013, Early

Years Teacher Status (EYTS) replaced EYPS. This shift in name and focus was intended to suggest parity between practitioners gaining the status and qualified teachers in the school sector, and focused their leadership of practice on 'teaching' in the early years sector. With this status came a new, and almost inevitably longer, set of standards – the Teacher's Standards (Early Years). The change in name marks a shift towards leading pedagogy, rather than the broader notion of practice, but it remains set within similar policy concerns. Policy makers have accepted the association between a higher level of staff qualifications and better inspection results and agreed that increasing the number of graduate leaders is a key means of improving the quality of leadership in the sector. The next key policy objective, drawing on effectiveness leadership research, is to ensure that this new group of leaders concentrates its efforts on those activities that are likely to have the most impact. Hence, the Teachers' Standards (Early Years) echo the EYPS Standards[1] in that these new early years leaders will:

2.4 Lead and model effective strategies to develop and extend children's learning and thinking, including sustained shared thinking.

8.4 Model and implement effective education and care, and support and lead other practitioners including Early Years Educators.

8.5 Take responsibility for leading practice through appropriate professional development for self and colleagues.

8.6 Reflect on and evaluate the effectiveness of provision, and shape and support good practice.[2]

In policy terms, practice leaders are therefore still expected to focus on modelling, developing and evaluating effective practice. What has slipped into the policy discourse is the recognition of the importance of building collective agency into any improvement initiative, although the Standards are fairly vague in their suggestion that Early Year Teachers should: 'Take a lead in establishing a culture of cooperative working between colleagues, parents and/or carers and other professionals.'[3]

In one sense, the shift represented by the introduction of Early Years Teacher Status is relatively minor: there is a greater focus on teaching and pedagogy and a requirement to ensure that certain areas of curriculum content are covered and even taught in specific ways. In the immediate future, the main impact of policy on practice leadership will be to keep it at the forefront of leadership development and training. The emphasis on effective practice is likely to lead to greater engagement with the current knowledge base in such programmes while also encouraging more emphasis to be placed on evaluating the impact of any innovations.

In the medium term, at least in England, if the policy agenda follows a similar arc to that of school leadership, it is likely to place increasing emphasis on system level reform based on generating leadership capacity throughout the sector. This would require different tiers of leadership to be developed, using models based on the notion of tri-level reform. Such leaders would be encouraged into formal and informal mentoring networks, with leadership development programmes being commissioned centrally and delivered locally. This sort of approach aims to encourage greater collaborative learning between individuals and settings and often sees a rise in leaders using broad enquiry approaches based upon tackling 'real' problems. In the medium term, the major policy impact on practice leadership is likely to be through the expansion of leadership development activities in the sector. If these activities maintain their focus on issues of effectiveness, improvement and quality, they are therefore likely to develop increased practice leadership capacity both in settings and in the sector as a whole.

Practitioners and practice leadership

One of the key outcomes of leaders' engagement with EYPS was that it increased their confidence in what they believed to be quality provision and in articulating their views to colleagues and parents: *'Because my knowledge is greater and my confidence in myself is greater, I feel more comfortable with a broad range of things that I can pass on to the staff'* (Practice leader, LS08). This increase in professional confidence supported them in leading change in their settings and encouraged them to develop others to take greater leadership responsibilities. At the time of the research, much of the change agenda was shaped by the requirement to implement the Early Years Foundation Stage (EYFS) and, to a degree, this limited their engagement with the nature of what constituted 'quality'. As familiarity with the benefits and limitations of the EYFS grows and the confidence of practice leaders increases while they build up track records of successful intervention, one possible future scenario is that, despite the pressures of external inspection, official notions of quality provision, such as those contained in the Early Years Professional and Early Years Teacher Standards, will come under greater scrutiny.

The scrutiny of 'accepted' or official notions of quality will be accelerated by the increase in practice leadership capacity in settings, and the sector as a whole, as it facilitates greater communication and learning between leaders. To what extent this may develop a greater sense of collective professional identity among leaders in the relatively fragmented early years sector in England is difficult to forecast. A more likely outcome is that the enhanced ability of leaders to learn from each other's practice, especially across different settings, will lead to greater experimentation involving different approaches to improving practice. In the medium term, we are likely to see a much more vocal group of leaders in the early years sector who will not only be prepared to be critical of existing notions of quality but also increasingly confident about how to bring about improvement in a wide range of contexts. In the longer term, these developments might feed back into the policy arena. This may lead to more prescription as to how to lead in certain contexts, rather than merely specifying what needs to be the focus of practice leadership.

Research and practice leadership

As we have discussed throughout the book, in an era of meta-syntheses, matched sample designs and systematic reviews, we are starting to build a more robust knowledge base about the key links in the chain between leadership and outcomes for children. Such work in the early years sector has been underpinned by major studies such as EPPE and REPEY. This book in part represents the next steps in the research agenda as we try to move from lists of generic characteristics of effective leaders to consider how, in one specific strand of activity – practice leadership – leaders brought about change that resulted in improved outcomes for children. Our conceptualisation of the links between leaders and outcomes was founded on the importance of the reciprocal relationship between leaders and the contexts in which they worked.

In developing this idea, we drew on the work of school effectiveness researchers who devised reciprocal logic models that explored the connections between changes in leadership approaches, developing schools' capacity for improvement, and outcomes for children. Currently, no work of a similar nature has been undertaken in the early years sector and the nature of the sector, particularly the size and dynamic nature of capacity in settings, presents complex challenges. The danger is that if research cannot match the methodological and theoretical sophistication of other sectors, rather than learning from such research, the early years sector could become overly reliant on research conceptualisations and findings that do not address this complexity.

Our approach to studying practice leadership drew on three mature research strands in the schools sector: effectiveness, improvement and leadership, combining them with the existing knowledge base from the early years sector. The future development of the idea of practice leadership in the early years requires these three strands to progress and interact. In the short term, there is a danger that leadership research will outstrip the other two strands, leading to the promotion of a plethora of styles and approaches that are not well grounded in evidence. A case in point is the already fashionable notion of more collaborative or distributed approaches to leadership. The danger here, as our own and others' research has shown, is that such approaches are only effective when a degree of leadership capacity already exists. Promoting such approaches without making this clear or without advising on how to build the necessary leadership capacity can result in disillusionment among practitioners about what has been shown to be a highly effective approach to improving outcomes for children.

In the medium term, the extent to which research in the early years shapes the idea of practice leadership will depend not only on the relative maturity of these three strands of research but also on how they interact. In the schools sector, even if they were not antagonistic to each other, they operated in isolation for many years. The problems faced by researchers in the schools sector need not be repeated in the early years. It is through recognising that each form of research introduces different kinds of insights, all of which are necessary to build a compelling argument, that evidence can emerge to challenge and support both practitioners and policy makers.

Notes

1   Teaching Agency (2012b) *Early Years Professional Status Standards (from September 2012)*. London: Teaching Agency.
2   National College for Teaching and Leadership (2013) *Teachers' Standards (Early Years)*. London: NCTL.
3   Ibid., at p. 5.

Appendix 1: Case study settings

Setting	Region	Type	EYPs	Deprivation range	Size
LS01	West Midlands	Children's centre	1	0–20%	Medium
LS03	West Midlands	Childminder	1	Over 80%	Small
LS04	West Midlands	Children's centre	4	0–20%	Medium
LS05	West Midlands	Children's centre	2	0–20%	Small
LS06	West Midlands	Voluntary/community	1	Over 80%	Small
LS08	North West	Children's centre	1	51–80%	Small
LS09	North West	Private	1	Over 80%	Small
LS11	North West	Private	1	21–50%	Small
LS12	North West	Private	1	0–20%	Large
LS13	North West	Private	1	0–20%	Large
LS14	North West	Private	1	0–20%	Medium
LS15	North West	Voluntary/community	1	0–20%	Small
LS17	North East	Children's centre	2	0–20%	Large
LS18	North East	Private	2	0–20%	Large
LS19	London/South East	Private	2	0–20%	Medium
LS20	London/South East	Children's centre	1	0–20%	Large
LS22	London/South East	Voluntary/community	1	0–20%	Small
LS24	London/South East	Private	2	21–50%	Small
LS28	East Midlands	Private	1	21–50%	Medium
LS29	East Midlands	Children's centre	3	21–50%	Large
LS30	East Midlands	Private	1	51–80%	Medium
LS32	North West	Childminder	1	51–80%	Small
LS35	East Midlands	Private	1	21–50%	Large
LS49	London/South East	Voluntary/community	1	21–50%	Medium
LS51	West Midlands	Children's centre	1	0–20%	Small
LS52	North West	Voluntary/community	1	21–50%	Small
LS53	East Midlands	Private	1	21–50%	Small
LS59	East	Children's centre	1	21–50%	Large
LS60	East	Children's centre	1	21–50%	Large
LS61	East Midlands	Independent	1	21–50%	Medium

Appendix 2: Sustained shared thinking interactions

Examples used in PCIT observations to identify sustained shared thinking.

Scaffolding An interaction that requires understanding of the child's level of knowledge and skills and scaffolds these through questions or comments in order to support the child to operate at a higher level than if he or she worked individually.

Clarifying ideas: 'Right Darren, so you think that this stone will melt if I boil it in water?'

Reminding: 'Don't forget that you said that this stone will melt if I boil it.'

Using encouragement to further thinking: 'You have really thought hard about where to put this door in the palace – where will you put the windows?'

Extrapolation: What else would do this?

Re-capping: 'So you think that . . .'

Anticipating: What do you think is going to happen next?

Formative feedback: This is about the particular qualities of the child's involvement in, or outcomes from, an activity with advice on what he or she can do to improve; comparisons with other pupils should be avoided.

Extending An interaction when the practitioner makes a suggestion to allow the child to see other possibilities.

Inviting children to elaborate: 'I really want to know more about this.'

Suggesting: 'You might like to try doing it this way.'

Offering an alternative viewpoint: 'Maybe Goldilocks wasn't naughty when she ate the porridge?'

Discussing   The practitioner has a prolonged discussion that is more than a series of questions and allows for the interchange of information or ideas.

Speculating: 'Do you think the three bears would have liked Goldilocks to come to live with them as their friend?'

Asking open questions: 'How did you?', 'Why does this . . .?', 'What happens next?', 'What do you think?'

Using positive questioning: 'I don't know, what do you think?', 'That's an interesting idea . . .', 'Have you seen what X has done – why?'

Modelling   The demonstration of activities accompanied by the child's attention and interest as well as a verbal commentary from the adult.

Offering the adult's own experience: 'I like to listen to music when I cook supper at home.'

Reciprocating: 'Thank goodness that you were wearing Wellington boots when you jumped in those puddles Kwame. Look at my feet, they are soaking wet!'

Modelling thinking: 'I have to think hard about what I do this evening. I need to take my dog to the vet because he has a sore foot, take my library books back to the library and buy some food for dinner tonight. But I just won't have time to do all of these things.'

References

Adams, K. (2008) What's in a name? Seeking professional status through degree studies within the Scottish early years context, *European Early Education Research Journal*, 16 (2), 196–209.

Adelman, C. (1993) Kurt Lewin and the origins of action research, *Educational Action Research*, 1 (1), 7–24.

Alderson, P. (2008) Children as researchers: participation rights and research methods, in P. Christensen and A. James (eds.) *Research with Children: Perspectives and practices*, 2nd edn. London: Routledge.

Anning, A., Cottrell, D., Frost, N., Green, J. and Robinson, M. (2006) *Developing Multiprofessional Teamwork for Integrated Children's Services: Research, policy and practice*. Maidenhead: Open University Press.

Anning, A., Cullen, J. and Fleer, M. (2009) *Early Childhood Education: Society and culture*, 2nd edn. London: Sage.

Aubrey, C. (2011) *Leading and Managing in the Early Years*, 2nd edn. London: Sage.

Aubrey, C., Godfrey, R. and Harris, A. (2013) How do they manage? An investigation of early childhood leadership, *Educational Management Administration and Leadership*, 41 (5), 5–29.

Balkundi, P. and Harrison, D.A. (2006) Ties, leaders, and time in teams: strong inference about the effects of network structure on team viability and performance, *Academy of Management Journal*, 49, 49–68.

Blanding, M. (2009) Treating the 'instructional core': education rounds. *Usable Knowledge*, 12 May. Cambridge, MA: Harvard Graduate School of Education.

Borgatti, S.P., Everett, M.G. and Freeman, L.C. (2002) *Ucinet for Windows: Software for social network analysis*. Harvard, MA: Analytic Technologies [http://www.gse.harvard.edu/news/uk/09/05/treating-instructional-core-education-rounds].

Britzman, D.P. (1992) Cultural myths in the making of a teacher: biography and social structure in teacher education, in M. Okazawa-Rey, J. Anderson and R. Traver (eds.) *Teachers, Teaching, and Teacher Education*. Cambridge, MA: Harvard Education Review.

Buono, A.F. and Kerber, K.W. (2008) The challenge of organizational change: enhancing organizational change capacity, *Revue Sciences de Gestion*, 65, 99–118.

Burchinal, M.R., Peisner-Feinberg, E., Bryant, D.M. and Clifford, R. (2000) Children's social and cognitive development and child care quality: testing for differential associations related to poverty, gender, or ethnicity, *Journal of Applied Developmental Sciences*, 4, 149–65.

Calderhead, J. (1981) Stimulated recall: a method for research in teaching, *British Journal of Educational Psychology*, 51 (2), 211–17.

Carr, M. and Lee, W. (2012) *Learning Stories: Constructing Learner Identities in Early Education*. London: Sage.

Children's Workforce Development Council (CWDC) (2006) *Early Years Professional Status Prospectus*. Leeds: CWDC.

Children's Workforce Development Council (CWDC) (2008) *Early Years Professional Status*. Leeds: CWDC.

Children's Workforce Development Council (CWDC) (2010) *On the Right Track: Guidance to the Standards for the Award of Early Years Professional Status*. Leeds: CWDC.

Chokshi, S. and Fernandez, C. (2004) Challenges to importing Japanese lesson study: concerns, misconceptions, and nuances, *Phi Delta Kappan*, 85 (7), 520–5.

City, E., Elmore, R., Fiarman, S. and Teitel, L. (2009) *Instructional Rounds in Education: A Network Approach to Improving Teaching and Learning*. Boston, MA: Harvard Education Press.

Clark, A. and Moss, P. (2001) *Listening to Young Children: The Mosaic Approach*. London: National Children's Bureau.

Clark, A. and Moss, P. (2005) *Spaces to Play: More Listening to Young Children Using the Mosaic Approach*. London: National Children's Bureau.

Coburn, C.E. and Russell, J.L. (2008) District policy and teachers' social networks, *Educational Evaluation and Policy Analysis*, 30 (3), 203–35.

Coleyshaw, L., Whitmarsh, J., Jopling, M. and Hadfield, M. (2012) *Listening to Children's Perspectives: Improving the Quality of Provision in Early Years Settings*. Research Report DFE-RR239b. London: DfE.

Cottle, M. and Alexander, E. (2012) Quality in early years settings: government, research and practitioners' perspectives, *British Educational Research Journal*, 38 (4), 635–54.

Dahlberg, G. and Moss, P. (2008) Beyond quality in early childhood education and care – languages of evaluation, *New Zealand Journal of Teachers' Work*, 5 (1), 3–12.

Daly, A.J. and Finnigan, K. (2010) A bridge between worlds: understanding network structure to understand change strategy, *Journal of Educational Change*, 11 (2), 111–38.

Daly, A., Moolenaar, N., Bolivar, J. and Burke, P. (2010) Relationships in reform: the role of teachers' social networks, *Journal of Educational Administration*, 48 (1), 359–91.

Davis, G. and Barry, A. (2013) Positive outcomes for children: early years professionals effecting change, *Early Child Development and Care*, 183 (1), 37–48.

Day, C. and Hadfield, M. (1996) Effectiveness and quality in continuing professional education: an empirical investigation of policy and practice in UK universities, *International Journal of Lifelong Education*, 15 (5), 370–81.

Day, C., Kington, A., Stobart, G. and Sammons, P. (2006) The personal and professional selves of teachers: stable and unstable identities, *British Educational Research Journal*, 32 (4), 601–16.

Department for Children, Schools and Families (DCSF) (2007) *The Children's Act: Building Brighter Futures*. London: DCSF.

Department for Children, Schools and Families (DCSF) (2008) *Building Brighter Futures: Next Steps for the Children's Workforce*. London: DCSF.

Department for Education (DfE) (2011) *Statutory Framework for the Early Years Foundation Stage*. London: DfE.

Department for Education (DfE) (2014a) *Early Years Pupil Premium and Funding for Two-year-olds*. London: DfE.

Department for Education (DfE) (2014b) *Statutory Framework for the Early Years Foundation Stage: Setting the Standards for Learning, Development and Care for Children from Birth to Five*. London: DfE.

Department for Education and Employment (DfEE) (2000) *Curriculum Guidance for the Foundation Stage*. London: Qualifications and Curriculum Authority.

Department for Education and Skills (DfES) (2004) *Children Act*. London: DfES.

Department for Education and Skills (DfES) (2005) *Children's Workforce Strategy: A Strategy to Build a World-class Workforce for Children and Young People*. London: DfES.

Department for Education and Skills (DfES) (2006a) *Childcare Act*. London: DfES.

Department for Education and Skills (DfES) (2006b) *Children's Workforce Strategy: Building a World-class Workforce for Children, Young People and Families – The Government's Response to the Consultation*. London: DfES.

Department for Education and Skills (DfES) (2007) *The Early Years Foundation Stage: Setting the Standards for Learning, Development and Care*. Nottingham: DfES.

Dudley, P. (2012) Lesson study in England: from school networks to national policy, *International Journal for Lesson and Learning Studies*, 1 (1), 85–100.

Fenech, M. (2011) An analysis of the conceptualisation of 'quality' in early childhood education and care empirical research: promoting 'blind spots' as foci for future research, *Contemporary Issues in Early Childhood*, 12 (2), 102–17.

Fenech, M. and Sumsion, J. (2007) Early childhood teachers and regulation: complicating power relations using a Foucauldian lens, *Contemporary Issues in Early Childhood*, 8 (2), 109–22.

Fullan, M. (2004) *Systems Thinkers in Action: Moving Beyond the Standards Plateau*. Nottingham: DfES.

Geijsel, F. and Meijers, F. (2005) Identity learning: the core process of educational change, *Educational Studies*, 31 (4), 419–30.

Giddens, A. (1984) *The Constitution of Society: Outline of the Theory of Structuration*. Berkeley, CA: University of California Press.

Goldman, P., Resnick, L., Bill, V., Johnston, J., Micheaux, D. and Seitz, A. (2004) *Learning Walk Source Book*. Pittsburgh, PA: Learning Research and Development Center.

Gronn, P. (2002) Distributed leadership as a unit of analysis, *Leadership Quarterly*, 13 (4), 423–51.

Gronn, P. (2008) The future of distributed leadership, *Journal of Educational Administration*, 46 (2), 141–58.

Gronn, P. (2011) Hybrid configurations of leadership, in A. Bryman, D. Collinson, K. Grint, B. Jackson and M. Uhl-Bien (eds.) *Sage Handbook of Leadership*. London: Sage.

Hadfield, M., Chapman, C., Curryer, I. and Barrett, P. (2001) *Capacity Building for Leadership and School Improvement*. Nottingham: National College for School Leadership.

Hadfield, M. and Hayes, M. (1993) A metaphysical approach to qualitative methodologies, *Educational Action Research*, 1 (1), 153–74.

Hadfield, M. and Jopling, M. (2012) *Second National Survey of Practitioners with Early Years Professional Status Report*. Research Report DFE-RR239a. London: DfE.

Hadfield, M., Jopling, M., Royle, K. and Waller, T. (2011) *First National Survey of Practitioners with Early Years Professional Status*. London: CWDC.

Hallet, E. and Roberts-Holmes, G. (2010) *The contribution of the Early Years Professional Status role to quality improvement strategies in Gloucestershire: Final Report*. Unpublished Manuscript, Institute of Education, University of London.

Hallinger, P. (2003) Leading educational change: reflections on the practice of instructional and transformational leadership, *Cambridge Journal of Education*, 33 (3), 329–51.

Hallinger, P. and Heck, R.H. (2011) Conceptual and methodological issues in studying school leadership effects as a reciprocal process, *School Effectiveness and School Improvement*, 22 (2), 149–73.

Hannah, S. and Lester, P. (2009) A multilevel approach to building and leading learning organizations, *The Leadership Quarterly*, 20, 34–48.

Hard, L. (2004) How is leadership understood in early childhood education and care?, *Journal of Australian Research in Early Childhood Education*, 11 (1), 123–31.

Hard, L. and Jónsdóttir, A.H. (2013) Leadership is not a dirty word: exploring and embracing leadership in ECEC, *European Early Childhood Education Research Journal*, 21 (3), 311–25.

Hargreaves, D.H. (2001) A capital theory of school effectiveness and improvement, *British Educational Research Journal*, 27 (4), 487–503.

Harms, T., Clifford, R. and Cryer, D. (1998) *Early Childhood Environment Rating Scale* (revised edn.). New York, NY: Teachers College Press.

Harms, T., Cryer, D. and Clifford, R.M. (2003) *Infant/Toddler Environment Rating Scale – Revised*. New York, NY: Teachers College Press.

Harris, A. (2004) Distributed leadership and school improvement: leading or misleading?, *Educational Management and Administration*, 32 (1), 11–24.

Harris, A. and Muijs, D. (2005) *Improving Schools through Teacher Leadership*. Maidenhead: Open University Press.

Hartley, D. (2007) The emergence of distributed leadership in education: why now?, *British Journal of Educational Studies*, 55 (2), 202–14.

Hartley, D. (2009) Paradigms: how far does research in distributed leadership 'stretch'?, *Educational Management Administration and Leadership*, 38 (3), 271–85.

Hatcher, R. (2005) The distribution of leadership and power in schools, *British Journal of Sociology of Education*, 26 (2), 253–67.

Heck, R.H. and Hallinger, P. (2010) Collaborative leadership effects on school improvement, *The Elementary School Journal*, 11 (2), 226–52.

Heikka, J. and Hujala, E. (2013) Early childhood leadership through the lens of distributed leadership, *European Early Childhood Education Research Journal*, 21 (4), 568–80.

Heikka, J. and Waniganayake, M. (2011) Pedagogical leadership from a distributed perspective within the context of early childhood education, *International Journal of Leadership in Education: Theory and Practice*, 14 (4), 499–512.

Heikka, J., Waniganayake, M. and Hujala, E. (2013) Contextualizing distributed leadership within early childhood education: current understandings, research evidence and future challenges, *Educational Management Administration and Leadership*, 41 (1), 30–44.

Hevey, D. (2010) Developing a new profession: a case study, *Literacy Information and Computer Education Journal*, 1 (3), 159–67.

Hopkins, D. (2001) *School Improvement for Real*. London: RoutledgeFalmer.

Jones, C. and Pound, L. (2008) *Leadership and Management in the Early Years*. Maidenhead: Open University Press.

Kachur, S., Stout, J. and Edwards, C. (2013) *Engaging Teachers in Classroom Walkthroughs*. Alexandria, VA: ASCD.

Katz, L.G. (1995) *Talks with Teachers of Young Children: A Collection*. Norwood, NJ: Ablex.

Kennedy, A. (2005) Models of continuing professional development: a framework for analysis, *Journal of In-Service Education*, 31 (2), 235–50.

Kuisma, M. and Sandberg, A. (2008) Preschool teachers' and student teachers' thoughts about professionalism in Sweden, *European Education Research Journal*, 16 (2), 186–95.

Laevers, F. (ed.) (1994) *Well-being and Involvement in Care Settings: A Process-oriented Self-evaluation Instrument*. Leuven: Research Centre for Experiential Education, University of Leuven.

Lewis, C., Perry, R. and Hurd, J. (2004) A deeper look at lesson study, *Educational Leadership*, 61 (5), 18–23.

Lindon, J. and Lindon, L. (2011) *Leadership and Early Years Professionalism: Linking Theory and Practice*. London: Hodder Education.

Lloyd, E. and Hallet, E. (2010) Professionalising the early childhood workforce in England: work in progress or missed opportunity?, *Contemporary Issues in Early Childhood*, 11 (1), 75–86.

Mathers, S., Ranns, H., Karemaker, A.M., Moody, A., Sylva, K., Graham, J. and Siraj-Blatchford, I. (2011) *Evaluation of Graduate Leader Fund: Final Report*. London: DfE.

Mathers, S. and Sylva, K. (2007) *National Evaluation of the Neighbourhood Nurseries Initiative: The Relationship between Quality and Children's Behavioural Development*. Research Report SSU/2007/FR/022. London: DfES.

Mathers, S., Sylva, K., Joshi, H., Hansen, K., Plewis, I., Johnson, J., George, A., Linskey, F. and Grabbe, Y. (2007) *Quality of Childcare Settings in the Millennium Cohort Study*. London: HMSO.

Maxwell, J. (2012) The importance of qualitative research for causal explanation in education, *Qualitative Inquiry*, 18 (8), 655–61.

McGillivray, G. (2011) Constructions of professional identity, in L. Miller and C. Cable (eds.) *Professionalization, Leadership and Management in the Early Years*. London: Sage.

Melhuish, E., Quinn, L., Hanna, K., Sylva, K., Siraj-Blatchford, I., Sammons, P. and Taggart, B. (2006) *The Effective Pre-school Provision in Northern Ireland Project, Summary Report*. Belfast: Stranmillis University Press.

Miller, L. (2008) Developing professionalism within a regulatory framework in England: challenges and possibilities, *European Early Childhood Education Research Journal*, 16 (2), 255–68.

Miller, M. and Cable, C. (eds.) (2008) *Professionalism in the Early Years Workforce*. London: Hodder.

Miller, M. and Cable, C. (eds.) (2011) *Professionalization, Leadership and Management in the Early Years*. London: Sage.

Mitchell, C. and Sackney, L. (2000) *Profound Improvement: Building Capacity for a Learning Community*. Lisse, Netherlands: Swets & Zeitlinger.

Mooney, A., Boddy, J., Statham, J. and Warwick, I. (2008) Approaches to developing health in early years settings, *Health Education*, 108 (2), 163–77.

Mooney, A., Cameron, C., Candappa, M., McQuail, S., Moss, P. and Petrie, P. (2003) *Early Years and Childcare International Evidence Project: Quality*. London: DfES.

Moss, P. and Pence, A. (eds.) (1994) *Valuing Quality in Early Childhood Services: New Approaches to Defining Quality*. London: Paul Chapman.

Moyles, J. (2006) *Effective Leadership and Management in the Early Years*. Maidenhead: Open University Press.

Muijs, D. (2011) Researching leadership: towards a new paradigm, in T. Townsend and J. MacBeath (eds.) *International Handbook of Leadership for Learning*, New York, NY: Springer.

Muijs, D., Aubrey, C., Harris, A. and Briggs, M. (2004) How do they manage? A review of the research on leadership in early childhood, *Journal of Early Childhood Research*, 2 (2), 157–69.

Munton, A.G., Mooney, A. and Rowland, L. (1995) Deconstructing quality: a conceptual framework for the new paradigm in day care provision for the under eights, *Early Childhood Development and Care*, 114, 11–23.

Murray, J. (2013) Becoming an early years professional: developing a new professional identity, *European Early Childhood Education Research Journal*, 21 (4), 527–40.

National College for Teaching and Leadership (2013) *Teachers' Standards (Early Years)*. London: NCTL.

Needham, M. (2013) *Early Years Professionals as Targeted Mentors for Leadership and Study: A Qualitative Review of Practitioners' Experiences of a Pilot Project in Shropshire*. Wolverhampton: University of Wolverhampton.

NICHD Early Child Care Research Network (2002) Early child care and children's development prior to school entry: results from the NICHD Study of Early Child Care, *American Educational Research Journal*, 39, 133–64.

Nurse, A. (2007) *The New Early Years Professionals*. London: Routledge.

Nutbrown, C. (2012) *Foundations for Quality: The Independent Review of Early Education and Childcare Qualifications. Final Report*. London: DfE.

Office for Standards in Education (Ofsted) (2008) *Early Years: Leading to Excellence*. London: Ofsted.

Pascal, C. and Bertram, T. (1997) *Effective Early Learning: Case Studies in Improvement*. London: Hodder & Stoughton.

Pascal, C., Bertram, A.D., Ramsden, F., Georgeson, J., Saunders, M. and Mould, C. (1996) *Evaluating and Developing Quality in Early Childhood Settings: A Professional Development Programme*. Worcester: Amber Publications.

Peisner-Feinberg, E.S. and Burchinal, M.R. (1997) Relations between preschool children's child-care experiences and concurrent development: the Cost, Quality, and Outcomes Study, *Journal of Developmental Psychology*, 43, 451–77.

Perry, R.R. and Lewis, C.C. (2009) What is successful adaptation of lesson study in the US?, *Journal of Educational Change*, 10 (4), 365–91.

Pitner, N. (1988) The study of administrator effects and effectiveness, in N. Boyan (ed.) *Handbook of Research in Educational Administration*. New York, NY: Longman.

Pyhalto, K., Pietarinen, J. and Soini, T. (2014) Comprehensive school teachers' professional agency in large-scale educational change, *Journal of Educational Change*, 15 (3), 303–25.

Resnick, L. (2010) Nested learning systems for the thinking curriculum, *Educational Researcher*, 39 (3), 183–97.

Reynolds, D. (1999) School effectiveness, school improvement and contemporary educational policies, in J. Demaine (ed.) *Contemporary Educational Policy and Politics*. London: Macmillan.

Roberts-Holmes, G. (2013) The English Early Years Professional Status (EYPS) and the 'split' Early Childhood Education and Care (ECEC) system, *European Early Childhood Education Research Journal*, 21 (3), 339–52.

Robinson, V.M. (2008) Forging the links between distributed leadership and educational outcomes, *Journal of Educational Administration*, 46 (2), 241–56.

Robinson, V., Hohepa, M. and Lloyd, C. (2009) *School Leadership and Student Outcomes: Identifying What Works and Why: Best Evidence Synthesis Iteration [BES]*. Wellington, NZ: Ministry of Education.

Rodd, J. (2006) *Leadership in Early Childhood: The Pathway to Professionalism*. Buckingham: Open University Press.

Sergiovanni, T.J. and Carver, F.D. (1980) *The New School Executive: A Theory of Administration*, 2nd edn. New York, NY: Harper & Row.

Sheridan, S. (2007) Dimensions of pedagogical quality in preschool, *International Journal of Early Years Education*, 15 (2), 197–217.

Siraj-Blatchford, I. (2009) Conceptualising progression in the pedagogy of play and sustained shared thinking, *Educational and Child Psychology*, 26 (2), 77–89.

Siraj-Blatchford, I., Clarke, K. and Needham, M. (eds.) (2007) *The Team Around the Child*. Stoke-on-Trent: Trentham Books.

Siraj-Blatchford, I. and Manni, L. (2007) *Effective Leadership in the Early Years Sector*. London: Institute of Education, University of London.

Siraj-Blatchford, I. and Sylva, K. (2004) Researching pedagogy in English pre-schools, *British Educational Research Journal*, 30 (5), 713–30.

Siraj-Blatchford, I., Sylva, K., Muttock, S., Gilden, R. and Bell, D. (2002) *Researching Effective Pedagogy in the Early Years*. Research Report DFES-RR356. London: DfES.

Siraj-Blatchford, I. and Wong, Y. (1999) Defining and evaluating quality in early childhood education in an international context: dilemmas and possibilities, *Early Years: An International Journal of Research and Development*, 20 (1), 7–18.

Southworth, G. (1998) *Leading Improving Primary Schools: The Work of Headteachers and Deputy Heads*. London: Falmer Press.

Southworth, G. (2004) *Primary School Leadership in Context: Leading Small, Medium and Large Sized Primary Schools*. London: Routledge Falmer.

Spillane, J.P., Diamond, J.B. and Jita, L. (2003) Leading instruction: the distribution of leadership for instruction, *Journal of Curriculum Studies*, 35 (5), 533–43.

Spillane, J.P., Halverson, R. and Diamond, J.B. (2001) Investigating school leadership practice, *Educational Researcher*, 30 (3), 23–8.

Spillane, J., Halverson, R. and Diamond, J. (2004) Towards a theory of leadership practice: a distributed perspective, *Journal of Curriculum Studies*, 36 (1), 3–34.

Spillane, J.P. and Kim, C.M. (2012) An exploratory analysis of formal school leaders' positioning in instructional advice and information networks in elementary schools, *American Journal of Education*, 119 (1), 73–102.

Sylva, K. (1994) School influences on children's development, *Child Psychology and Psychiatry*, 35 (1), 135–70.

Sylva, K. (2010) Quality in early childhood settings, in K. Sylva, E. Melhuish, P. Sammons, I. Siraj-Blatchford and B. Taggart (eds.) *Early Childhood Matters: Evidence from the Effective Pre-school and Primary Education Project.* London: Routledge.

Sylva, K., Melhuish, E., Sammons, P., Siraj-Blatchford, I. and Taggart, B. (2004) *The Final Report: Effective Pre-School Education.* Technical Paper 12: The Effective Provision of Pre-School Education (EPPE Project). London: Institute of Education, University of London/DfES.

Sylva, K., Melhuish, E., Sammons, P., Siraj-Blatchford, I. and Taggart, B. (2010) *Early Childhood Matters: Evidence from the Effective Pre-school and Primary Education* Project. London: Routledge.

Sylva, K., Siraj-Blatchford, I. and Taggart, B. (2003) *Assessing Quality in the Early Years: Early Childhood Environment Rating Scale-Extension (ECERS-E): Four Curricular Subscales.* Stoke-on Trent: Trentham Books.

Teaching Agency (2012a) *Review of the Early Years Professional Status Standards.* London: Teaching Agency.

Teaching Agency (2012b) *Early Years Professional Status Standards (from September 2012).* London: Teaching Agency.

Tickell, C. (2011) *The Early Years: Foundations for Life, Health and Learning. An Independent Report on the Early Years Foundation Stage by Her Majesty's Government.* London: National Archives.

TIMSS (1998) *Third International Trends in Mathematics and Science Study.* New Zealand: Comparative Education Research Unit.

Tobin, J. (2005) Quality in early childhood education: an anthropologist's perspective, *Early Education and Development*, 16 (4), 422–34.

Vandell, D.L. and Wolfe, B. (2000) Childcare quality: does it matter and does it need to be improved?, *Institute for Research on Poverty Special Report*, 78, 1–110.

Wellman, B. and Berkowitz, S. (eds.) (1988) *Social Structures: A Network Approach.* New York, NY: Cambridge University Press.

Whalley, M. (2008) *Leading Practice in Early Years Settings (Achieving EYPS).* Exeter: Learning Matters.

Whalley, M. (2011) Leading and managing in the early years, in L. Miller and C. Cable (eds.) *Professionalization, Leadership and Management in the Early Years.* London: Sage.

Yammarino, F.J., Dionne, S.D., Chun, J.U. and Dansereau, F. (2005) Leadership and levels of analysis: a state-of-the-science review, *The Leadership Quarterly*, 16 (6), 879–919.

York-Barr, J. and Duke, K. (2004) What do we know about teacher leadership? Findings from two decades of scholarship, *Review of Educational Research*, 74 (3), 255–316.

Index

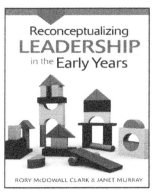

RECONCEPTUALIZING LEADERSHIP IN THE
EARLY YEARS

Rory McDowall Clark and Janet Murray

9780335246243 (Paperback)
August 2012

eBook also available

This book explores the realities of leadership in the early years and examines
the challenges and opportunities for the profession. The authors suggest that
recent moves to professionalize the workforce offer a unique opportunity to
reconceptualize leadership and develop a new paradigm more suited to the
specific circumstances of the sector.

Key features:

- Ideas based on research from a wide range of current early years
  practice
- Real leadership profiles of practitioners from a diversity of different
  professional backgrounds and working in a variety of contexts
- Reflective prompts to assist you in identifying the leadership in your
  own practice and how this can be developed further

OPEN UNIVERSITY PRESS
McGraw - Hill Education

www.openup.co.uk

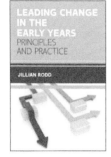

Leading Change in the Early Years

Jillian Rodd

ISBN: 978-0-335-26370-7 (Paperback)
eBook: 978-0-335-26371-4
2014

Leading Change in the Early Years focuses on the type of leadership skill needed for leading the reform and change agendas that challenge the early years sector. Early years professionals are expected to implement a range of government initiatives, as well as professionally endorsed changes, aimed at raising the quality of early years provision.

Key features include:

- Understanding the link between competent leadership and successful change
- Explores the dimensions, models and processes of change
- Explores the strategies for reducing reluctance and resistance

www.openup.co.uk

OPEN UNIVERSITY PRESS
McGraw · Hill Education